■SCHOLASTIC

Grades 5–6

Standardized Test Practice
LONG READING PASSAGES

16 Reproducible Passages With Test-Format Questions
That Help Students Succeed on Standardized Tests

Michael Priestley

D1403769

New York • Toronto • London • Auckland • Sydney
Mexico City • New Delhi • Hong Kong • Buenos Aires

Teaching *Resources*

Edited by Mela Ottaiano
Cover design by Brian LaRossa
Interior design by Creative Pages, Inc.
Illustrations by Wilkinson Studios, Inc.
ISBN-13: 978-0-545-08333-1
ISBN-10: 0-545-08333-8

4 5 6 7 8 9 10   40   15

Contents

Introduction

Many statewide assessments and standardized tests now feature a greater variety of reading passages and passages of greater length than in the past. It is not uncommon for students to encounter reading passages that are four, five, or even six pages long. In addition to longer passages, many tests now include both multiple-choice and written-response questions, which may be worth 2 to 4 points.

Students are more likely to succeed on tests like these if they experience this kind of challenging comprehension task beforehand. That's the main purpose of this book: to help prepare students for reading and responding to longer reading passages.

How to Use This Book

This book provides 16 reading passages (both prose and poetry) ranging from two to four pages in length—and from Grade 5 to Grade 6 in reading level. Each passage has 6 to 10 questions, including both multiple-choice and written-response. You may want to have students work through all of the 16 passages in sequence, or you may use them in any order. For example, you might choose passages that relate to the subject-area content that you are covering in class at a given time.

- For each passage that you choose, make a copy of the passage and the questions for each student.

- Have students read the passage and then answer the questions on the page—by marking the answer circles or writing their answers on the lines provided.

- After students have answered all of the questions, you can score their responses by referring to the answer key at the back of this book.

- You and your students may want to monitor their progress by recording their scores on the Student Scoring Record (page 96).

The answer key gives the correct answers to multiple-choice questions and example responses for written-response questions. In addition, the answer key indicates the reading comprehension or vocabulary skill tested by each question. You may find this information useful when evaluating which questions students answered incorrectly and planning for the kinds of instructional help they may need.

Scoring Responses

The comprehension practice activities in this book include multiple-choice items and two kinds of written-response questions. Each multiple-choice item is worth 1 point. Written-response questions may be worth 2 points or 4 points. (The number of points is indicated in parentheses at the end of the question.) Two-point responses generally require two parts or two pieces of information. Four-point responses generally require four parts or four pieces of information. Requirements and the point value for these responses are outlined in the answer key. You may award full or partial credit for a student's written response to a question. For example, on a 4-point question, students may earn 0, 1, 2, 3, or 4 points for a response, which follows the method of most standardized tests.

Name _____ Date _____

Directions: Read "Andruw's Latest Scheme." Then answer questions 1–6.

Andruw's Latest Scheme

Andruw Lee put his head down on the kitchen table and moaned. All his efforts to make money had failed, and his most recent enterprise was becoming a disaster.

It all started when his parents refused to raise his allowance. They just didn't understand that a guy in middle school has more expenses than he had in elementary school. They said that if Andruw wanted more money, he would need to earn it. So, fine, he would earn it.

The problem was that nothing Andruw had tried so far had worked out. Among other problems, his options were limited. There just weren't that many legitimate ways for a kid his age to make money. His dad was always talking to him about paper routes, but these days newspapers were delivered by adults in cars or downloaded from the Internet. He couldn't help people paint their houses because all the houses had vinyl siding, which doesn't need painting. The stores were too far away for running errands. He was too young to baby-sit at night, and nobody needed sitters after school.

In theory, he could do yard work. However, leaf raking and snow shoveling were both months away. Lawn mowing, the big moneymaker, was also out. His parents made him cut their own grass but wouldn't let him mow for the neighbors. (They seemed to think he'd be more likely to run over his own foot without one of them hovering nearby.) That pretty much left gardening, which he had tried. His one customer was very satisfied after he raked her garden and unloaded bags of topsoil from her car. Then one day when he weeded out all her vegetable seedlings by accident, his employer gently fired him. She commented that perhaps gardening was not his strength.

Following his failure as a gardener, Andruw had marketed himself as a pet sitter and dog walker. That worked pretty well for a while. He didn't walk any dogs, but neighbors who went out of town on weekends hired him to feed their tropical fish. Andruw took his job seriously. He was very careful to measure the right amounts of food. He checked the temperature of the tank and added water as needed. Everything was fine until one night the neighbors' power went off and all the fish met an untimely fate. That was the end of that.

Forget about having a lemonade stand. This wasn't the 1950s. But the thought of lemonade had led to Andruw's next scheme (and his current calamity). Reaching for a cold drink, Andruw was suddenly hit by the idea of refrigerator magnets. He could make and sell *customized jigsaw puzzle* refrigerator magnets! His customers could give him pictures they liked. He could scan them into the computer and print them out. He'd glue the printouts onto oversize magnets, which he could buy at the craft store. Then he'd cut the magnets into puzzle pieces. People could use the pieces separately as magnets or put them together like a puzzle. Rather than setting up a stand, he could market his product door-to-door in the neighborhood. He could take orders from his friends and teachers. His grandmother in Iowa would surely want one. What a great idea!

Andruw invested all his fish-sitting money in magnets and special printing paper. Then he started taking orders. Then he got more orders, and more orders. As word got out, Andruw's sales soared. Everyone wanted one of his magnets. His locker at school was soon filled with pictures to be turned into magnets. The trouble was, a lot of the pictures had no names written on them. He couldn't remember which image went with which person. He should have made order forms.

The next problem was scanning and printing the pictures. This task took a lot of time, and he had to keep stopping so his brother could use the computer. Then the printer ran out of ink in the middle of the job. He had to get his mom to take him to the store for a new printer cartridge. She made him pay for it, too, although she did agree to lend him the money until his customers paid for their magnets.

That was part of the disaster. In deciding how much to charge, Andruw had figured in the cost of the magnets and paper, but not the ink or glue. There was only one kind of glue he could find that would stick to the magnets, and it was expensive. At the price he had quoted his customers, Andruw was going to lose money on each magnet.

The other part of the disaster was the slow construction process. Producing a good print took a long time. Carefully gluing the print to the magnet took even longer. On top of everything else, he had to keep stopping to clean his blade because the glue gummed it up. His first round of orders took so long that Andruw had no time for anything else except eating, sleeping, and school. Even if he had made a profit, he had no time to spend the money.

So here he was with his head on the table, trying to think. What was he going to do? Life in middle school was passing him by while he was stuck at home, up to his elbows in glue.

As Andruw anguished over his situation, his parents came into the room and sat down. Andruw braced himself for a lecture, but instead they told him they were proud of him. They said they realized he had tried very hard and were sorry his efforts had not succeeded. They thought he had probably learned some valuable lessons. Now they were prepared to help him out. Once he filled the orders for his current customers, they would increase his allowance a little. They would also help him figure out ways to earn more money if he needed it.

But, they added, he still owed his mom for the printer cartridge.

Questions 1–6: Choose the best answer to each question, or write your answer on the lines provided.

1. **Putting his head down on the table shows that Andruw was feeling —**

   Ⓐ sleepy.

   Ⓑ frightened.

   Ⓒ bored.

   Ⓓ discouraged.

2. **Why didn't Andruw's parents agree to raise his allowance when he asked?**

   Ⓐ They thought he was wasting money on his projects.

   Ⓑ They felt he was already getting enough allowance.

   Ⓒ They didn't have enough money to give him more.

   Ⓓ They wanted him to spend more time studying.

3. **Which of these money-making schemes did Andruw try first?**

   Ⓐ painting

   Ⓑ baby-sitting

   Ⓒ gardening

   Ⓓ pet-sitting

Standardized Test Practice: Long Reading Passages (Grades 5–6) © 2009 by Michael Priestley, Scholastic Teaching Resources

4. **Read this sentence from the passage.**

> Life in middle school was passing him by while he was stuck at home, <u>up to his elbows in glue.</u>

What does it mean to say that Andruw was <u>up to his elbows in glue?</u>

(A) He had glue on his sleeves.

(B) It was hard to get the glue out of the tube.

(C) The glue was very expensive.

(D) He was working with lots of glue.

5. **What can you conclude from Andruw's experiences as a pet sitter?**

(A) Not all of Andruw's failures were his fault.

(B) Pet-sitting is not a good way for kids to make money.

(C) The idea for the magnet project came from pet-sitting.

(D) Andruw never finished any of the jobs he started.

6. **What kind of person is Andruw? Use details from the passage to support your answer. (2 points)**

_____

_____

_____

_____

Standardized Test Practice: Long Reading Passages (Grades 5–6) © 2009 by Michael Priestley, Scholastic Teaching Resources

Name _____ Date _____

Directions: Read "Shirley Chisholm: A Political Pioneer." Then answer questions 1–7.

Shirley Chisholm: A Political Pioneer

In the 2008 presidential race, two leading candidates for the Democrats included an African American and a woman. In talking about the campaign, many people said it was the first time that a woman and a black person had tried for the White House at the same time. But that's not exactly true. In 1972, one person who ran for president was both black and a woman. That political pioneer was Shirley Chisholm of New York.

Chisholm's early life shaped her later views on politics. She was born in Brooklyn, New York, in 1924. Her father was an immigrant from Guyana who worked in a burlap bag factory. Her mother was from Barbados and worked as a maid. Her parents were poor, and they wanted Shirley to have a better life. When she was three years old, they sent her to live with relatives in Barbados. Shirley went to school there and gained a love for education that would last her whole life. She moved back to Brooklyn in 1934 at the age of 10. After high school, she went on to graduate with honors from Brooklyn College (1946). Then, in 1951, she earned a master's degree from Columbia University Teachers College.

For a number of years, Chisholm worked as a teacher and as a director at day care centers in New York City. Then she became an education consultant for the city's Bureau of Child Welfare, a post she held from 1959 to 1964.

During this time, Chisholm was becoming involved in politics. She volunteered with the League of Women Voters. She also worked for local candidates. In 1964, she ran for office herself and was elected to the New York State Assembly. She served there from 1964 to 1968. During her term, she worked for better education. She backed bills to improve day care and increase funding for schools in the state.

In 1968, Chisholm was elected to the U.S. House of Representatives. She was the first African-American woman to serve in Congress. "Just wait," she said as she headed off to Washington, "there may be some fireworks."

Sure enough, Chisholm began to shake things up as soon as she arrived. Most new members of Congress have little say about the committees they work on. Chisholm was assigned to the Agriculture Committee, but that made no sense. Her district was in the middle of one of America's biggest cities. Instead of keeping quiet, she challenged her assignment. As a result, she was moved to the Veterans' Affairs Committee. Later, she served on the Education and Labor Committee and the House Rules Committee.

During her time in Congress, Chisholm became known as a skilled speaker. She was also a fierce champion for the poor, women, children, and minorities. In order to give these groups a greater voice, she helped found the Congressional Black Caucus in 1969. Then she helped found the National Women's Political Caucus in 1971.

Shirley Chisholm was not afraid of making people upset. She did what she thought was right. One famous example was a visit she made in 1972 to Governor George Wallace of Alabama. Wallace had fought hard against the civil rights movement. But he was shot while running for president, and Chisholm visited him. She knew many would be shocked by this act of concern, but that did not stop her. (As it turned out, Wallace later helped Chisholm gain support for a bill she was backing. But she didn't know that would happen at the time.)

In 1972, Chisholm ran for president. She did not win any states in the primary elections. But she won enough votes to allow her to speak at the Democratic convention. In doing so, she earned another "first." She gave a remarkable speech at the convention and earned a lot of attention. As she wrote in a 1973 book about her experiences, "The next time a woman runs, or a black, a Jew, or anyone from a group that the country is 'not ready' to elect to its highest office, I believe that he or she will be taken seriously from the start."

Chisholm served in Congress for seven terms. After she retired in 1983, she taught at Mount Holyoke and Spelman colleges. She was also in great demand as a public speaker.

Chisholm died in 2005 at the age of 80. Her obituaries recalled that she had once been asked how she would like to be remembered. She replied, "I'd like them to say that Shirley Chisholm had guts."

Today, a lot of people do not know about Chisholm and the doors she opened for so many (including those 2008 candidates). In a way, what seemed "gutsy" in 1972 has become more common today. Shirley Chisholm would certainly view that as a sign of progress.

Standardized Test Practice: Long Reading Passages (Grades 5–6) © 2009 by Michael Priestley, Scholastic Teaching Resources

Questions 1–7: Choose the best answer to each question, or write your answer on the lines provided.

1. **What is this passage mostly about?**

   Ⓐ people who ran for president in 2008

   Ⓑ education and day care in New York City

   Ⓒ Shirley Chisholm's meeting with George Wallace

   Ⓓ the life and career of Shirley Chisholm

2. **Information in this passage is organized mainly by —**

   Ⓐ cause and effect.

   Ⓑ order of importance.

   Ⓒ problem and solution.

   Ⓓ chronological order.

3. **Read this sentence from the passage.**

   She was also a <u>fierce</u> champion for the poor, women, children, and minorities.

   What does the word <u>fierce</u> suggest about Chisholm?

   Ⓐ She fought hard for what she wanted.

   Ⓑ She was a violent person.

   Ⓒ She became angry when she did not win.

   Ⓓ She had bad manners.

4. **Which statement about Shirley Chisholm is an opinion?**

   Ⓐ She made a famous visit to Governor George Wallace.

   Ⓑ She gave a remarkable speech at the convention.

   Ⓒ She was the first African-American woman to serve in Congress.

   Ⓓ She taught at Mt. Holyoke and Spelman colleges.

5. The passage says, "Chisholm's early life shaped her later views on politics."

Which evidence from the passage best supports this statement?

Ⓐ Her parents were immigrants; she later worked on immigration issues.

Ⓑ She was born in Brooklyn; she later represented Brooklyn in Congress.

Ⓒ Her parents were poor; she later stood up for poor people in Congress.

Ⓓ She graduated from college with honors; she later ran for president.

6. Using information from the passage, explain why Shirley Chisholm was a "political pioneer." (2 points)

_____

_____

_____

_____

7. If you wanted to learn more about Shirley Chisholm, which would be the best source of information?

Ⓐ an almanac

Ⓑ an online encyclopedia

Ⓒ a dictionary

Ⓓ a weekly news magazine

Standardized Test Practice: Long Reading Passages (Grades 5–6) © 2009 by Michael Priestley, Scholastic Teaching Resources

Name _____ Date _____

Directions: Read "Deserts of the United States." Then answer questions 1–8.

Deserts of the United States

What do you think of when you hear the word *desert*? You might think of hot temperatures and dry weather. You might think of a large cactus reaching toward the sky. These are common features of deserts. However, there are some things you may not know about deserts. For example, many deserts have abundant animal and plant life, and some even receive snow during the winter.

The United States has four deserts. Can you name them? They are the Great Basin, the Mojave, the Sonoran, and the Chihuahuan. Each of these deserts has its own characteristics and features. But they all have one thing in common: they are dry. Deserts generally get less than 10 inches of rain per year.

The Great Basin

The Great Basin is unique. Do you know why? It is the only cold desert in the United States. This land area receives 60 percent of its precipitation as snow. The Great Basin is located in the western part of the United States, mainly in Nevada. Parts of this desert also extend into Utah, Idaho, Oregon, and California. It was once home to many large lakes, but these have mostly dried up. Most of those lakes were salty—even saltier than the ocean. As a result, the soil left behind is very salty. It is not well suited for vegetation. Some plants, such as sagebrush and greasewood, have adapted to this saline soil and thrive in the Great Basin. But there are very few cacti in this desert.

The Sonoran Desert

Across southern California, southwestern Arizona, and into Mexico lies the Sonoran Desert. This desert gets rain in both the summer and the winter, which leads to plentiful and diverse plant life. However, it is still quite dry. It has an annual rainfall of 4 to 12 inches, depending on the side of the desert.

Standardized Test Practice: Long Reading Passages (Grades 5–6) © 2009 by Michael Priestley, Scholastic Teaching Resources

One of the most exciting sights in the Sonoran Desert is the stately saguaro cactus. Did you know that this magnificent plant can grow to reach 50 feet? But it takes quite a long time to reach such great heights. The saguaro only grows a few inches a year. After 30 years, it may only be a few feet high. It takes two centuries (200 years) for the saguaro to reach its full height. The saguaro will also grow "arms," but the first arm doesn't form until the cactus is at least 50 years old. Since it grows so slowly, the saguaro requires little food and water. This makes it a perfect match for a dry desert location.

The Mojave Desert

The Mojave Desert is the smallest desert of the four. It is located between the Great Basin and the Sonoran Desert. It does not receive as much precipitation as the other deserts. In fact, it is the driest desert in the United States. It receives most of its precipitation—4 to 6 inches a year—in the winter months. Death Valley, California, is located in the Mojave, and it lives up to its name. It is the hottest place in the country. The highest temperature ever recorded there was a sweltering 134 degrees Fahrenheit!

When you hear the name Mojave, what do you think of? Many people think of the Joshua tree. This yucca plant is plentiful in the Mojave and is considered the desert's symbol. Like the saguaro, the Joshua tree has large arms that bend and extend outward. The leaves are spike-shaped and extend off the arms. These leaves help insulate the Joshua tree against the heat of the sun. They also help hold in moisture, which is sparse in the Mojave.

The Chihuahuan Desert

Most of the Chihuahuan Desert lies in Mexico, but a small portion is located in the United States (in New Mexico, Arizona, and Texas). This desert has many mountains that are 3,000 to 6,000 feet tall. It is the easternmost and southernmost of the four deserts. The winters can be cool, and freezing conditions are common in the northern part of the desert because of the high altitude. Plants that cannot survive in the cold are found in the southernmost regions of the desert. As you travel toward the north, these plants become fewer in number. Unlike the Sonoran or the Mojave, the Chihuahuan is mainly a shrub and grass desert. You won't find any tall trees or cacti here.

Now that you've learned more information about deserts, which one appeals to you the most? If you'd like to see snow in the desert, head to the Great Basin. If you want to see the most varied animal and plant life, take a trip to the Sonoran. However, no matter which one you visit, be sure to bring lots of water!

Questions 1–8: Choose the best answer to each question, or write your answer on the lines provided.

1. **What is a likely reason that most trees are unable to grow in the Great Basin?**
   - (A) The ground is too wet.
   - (B) The soil is too salty.
   - (C) There are too many mountains.
   - (D) There is not enough precipitation.

2. **Which desert has the highest temperatures?**
   - (A) Great Basin
   - (B) Sonoran
   - (C) Mojave
   - (D) Chihuahuan

3. **How are the Joshua tree and the saguaro cactus similar?**
   - (A) They both grow a few inches per year.
   - (B) They both can grow to 50 feet tall.
   - (C) They both have spiny leaves.
   - (D) They both grow arms.

Standardized Test Practice: Long Reading Passages (Grades 5–6) © 2009 by Michael Priestley, Scholastic Teaching Resources

4. **Most of the information in this passage is organized by —**

Ⓐ comparison and contrast.

Ⓑ cause and effect.

Ⓒ problem and solution.

Ⓓ chronological order.

5. **Describe the plant life in each of the four deserts. (4 points)**

_____

_____

_____

_____

_____

_____

_____

_____

6. **"Many plants have adapted to this <u>saline</u> soil and thrive in the Great Basin."**

What is the meaning of the word <u>saline</u>?

Ⓐ very healthy

Ⓑ containing salt

Ⓒ offered for sale

Ⓓ rich and moist

7. **Which sentence from the passage states an opinion?**

Ⓐ Each of these deserts has its own characteristics.

Ⓑ Deserts generally get less than 10 inches of rain per year.

Ⓒ One of the most exciting sights in the Sonoran Desert is the stately saguaro cactus.

Ⓓ The saguaro will also grow "arms," but the first arm doesn't form until the cactus is at least 50 years old.

8. **The author of this passage tries to make it more interesting to the reader by —**

Ⓐ using unusual words to describe deserts.

Ⓑ trying to convince the reader to take a trip.

Ⓒ telling the reader entertaining stories.

Ⓓ asking the reader questions.

Standardized Test Practice: Long Reading Passages (Grades 5–6) © 2009 by Michael Priestley, Scholastic Teaching Resources

Name _____ Date _____

Directions: Read "How Sun, Moon, and Wind Went to Dinner."
Then answer questions 1–6.

How Sun, Moon, and Wind Went to Dinner

One day Sun, Moon, and Wind went to dine with their uncle and aunt, Thunder and Lightning. Their mother (one of the most distant stars you see far up in the sky) waited alone for her children's return.

Now both Sun and Wind were greedy and selfish. They savored the great feast that had been prepared for them without a thought of saving any of it to take home to their mother. But gentle Moon did not forget her. Of every delicious dish that was brought around, she saved a small portion. She hid these tasty morsels under her long, beautiful fingernails so that their mother, Star, might share in the treat.

On their return, their mother, who had kept watch for them all night long with her silver bright eye, said hopefully, "Well, children, what wonderful treats have you brought home for me?"

Sun (who was eldest) said, "I have brought nothing home for you. I went out to enjoy myself, not to fetch a dinner for my mother!"

And Wind said, "Neither have I brought anything home for you, Mother. You could hardly expect me to bring home good things for you when I merely went out for my own pleasure."

But Moon said, "Mother, let me fetch a plate, and you will see what I have brought you." Then, shaking her fingers, she showered down a splendid dinner of the most wonderful foods.

When Star saw what Moon had brought, she was pleased with her youngest child. But Sun and Wind had let her down. She turned to Sun and said, "So, you went out to amuse yourself. Because you feasted and enjoyed yourself without any thought of your mother at home, you shall be cursed. Henceforth, your rays shall forever be hot and scorching, and shall burn all that they touch. Men and women shall despise you and cover their heads when you appear."

And that is why the Sun is so hot to this day.

Then she turned to Wind and said, "You who also forgot your mother in the midst of your selfish pleasures, hear your doom. You shall always blow in the hot dry weather and shall parch and shrivel all living things. People shall detest and avoid you from this very time."

And that is why the Wind during spells of hot weather is still so disagreeable.

But to Moon she said, "Daughter, you are the only one who remembered your mother and cared enough to share your own enjoyment. From this day forth, you shall be ever cool and calm and bright. No damaging glare shall accompany your marvelous light, and people shall always consider you precious."

And that is why the Moon's light is so soft and cool and beautiful even to this day.

Standardized Test Practice: Long Reading Passages (Grades 5–6) © 2009 by Michael Priestley, Scholastic Teaching Resources

Standardized Test Practice: Long Reading Passages (Grades 5–6) © 2009 by Michael Priestley, Scholastic Teaching Resources

Name _____   Date _____

Questions 1–6: Choose the best answer to each question, or write your answer on the lines provided.

1. **Who is the narrator of this passage?**

   Ⓐ a star

   Ⓑ the moon

   Ⓒ an outside observer

   Ⓓ thunder and lightning

2. **"They <u>savored</u> the great feast that had been prepared for them."**

   Which word is a synonym for <u>savored</u>?

   Ⓐ enjoyed

   Ⓑ cleared

   Ⓒ accepted

   Ⓓ spoiled

3. **How can you tell that this passage is a myth?**

   Ⓐ It uses figurative language to tell a story.

   Ⓑ It uses a fictional story to explain why natural events occur.

   Ⓒ It describes important events in a person's life.

   Ⓓ It has characters but no clear setting.

4. **Complete the sequence chart below with details from the passage. (4 points)**

Events in the Plot
1. Sun, Moon, and Wind go out to dinner.
2.
3.
4. Star curses Sun and Wind forever, but she blesses Moon for being so thoughtful.

5. **How do Star's feelings change in this passage when Sun, Moon, and Wind return from dinner?**

Ⓐ She is worried at first but then relieved.

Ⓑ She is angry at first but then confused.

Ⓒ She is sad at first but then happy.

Ⓓ She is hopeful at first but then disappointed.

6. **What is the theme of this story?**

Ⓐ Good friends are hard to find.

Ⓑ Treat others as you want them to treat you.

Ⓒ You must make sacrifices to get what you want.

Ⓓ You won't get what you want unless you ask.

Standardized Test Practice: Long Reading Passages (Grades 5–6) © 2009 by Michael Priestley, Scholastic Teaching Resources

Name _____ Date _____

Standardized Test Practice: Long Reading Passages (Grades 5–6) © 2009 by Michael Priestley, Scholastic Teaching Resources

Directions: Read "Natural Disasters." Then answer questions 1–8.

Natural Disasters

Our planet can be a calm place, but weather conditions often change rapidly. Gentle breezes can blow into fierce and howling winds. Light snow flurries can become ferocious winter storms. Gentle rains can turn into flooding downpours. The weather can be very powerful.

A natural disaster is a weather-related event that creates dangerous and destructive conditions. It is important to learn about natural disasters so you can be prepared if you face one. There are several kinds of natural disasters that may occur in the United States each year, and each one poses significant dangers.

Hurricanes

A hurricane is a huge storm that forms over warm ocean water. Bands of thunderstorms form and swirl around and around because of the rotation of the earth. As more and more thunderstorms form, the hurricane gets bigger and bigger. A hurricane is one of the world's worst storms because it can last for days or weeks. Hurricanes can also be very large. They may cover hundreds of miles and affect large areas of land.

For a storm to be classified as a hurricane, wind speeds within the storm have to reach at least 74 miles per hour. But hurricane winds can reach speeds of over 155 miles per hour! A large amount of destruction may occur with winds that strong. Roofs may be torn off houses. Buildings may be flattened. Trees topple over. Hurricanes are deadly, but not just because of their winds. They can also produce very heavy rains and huge waves that slam into the coastline.

Hurricanes are very common along the east coast of the United States. Here, wind, waves, and rain do the most damage. However, since hurricanes are so large, people who live 100 miles inland may also feel the effects of the wind and rain and sustain damage to their property.

Luckily, meteorologists (people who study weather) can forecast hurricanes days in advance by using radar technology. Radar is a little bit like a moving picture. It shows how big storms are and which way they are moving. Radar images give people time to prepare for a coming storm. If the storm is very strong, home and business owners will put up plywood to protect their glass windows and doors. People who live along the coast will evacuate. They'll go to a hurricane shelter or stay with friends and relatives who live in safer places farther inland. Many lives are saved every year by people who take the necessary precautions.

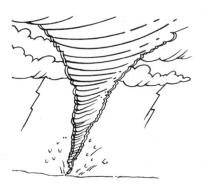

Tornadoes

Nothing is more frightening than a tornado. A tornado is a huge tower of moist, warm circling air. It usually develops during a strong thunderstorm. A column of clouds will form and reach down toward the ground. This is called a funnel cloud. It becomes a tornado when the cloud reaches the ground.

Tornadoes move at a high rate of speed and usually destroy buildings, trees, and anything else in their path. While a tornado is turning, it can also suck large objects into it, such as houses and cars. Wind speeds in a tornado may reach 300 miles per hour! Luckily, almost 70 percent of tornadoes are categorized as "weak" tornadoes with winds less than 110 miles per hour. Weak tornadoes usually last only 1–10 minutes, compared with hurricanes that can last for days or weeks. Still, these storms can do a lot of damage.

Tornadoes are most common in the Midwestern United States where the land is flat. But, wherever there is a strong thunderstorm, a tornado can occur. In 1984, for example, there were 22 tornadoes that formed from thunderstorms near the east coast in North and South Carolina. These tornadoes killed almost 60 people and injured over 1,000.

Unlike hurricanes, tornadoes are not easy to predict. People may only have a few minutes of warning when a tornado forms in their area. Usually, forecasters will place an area under a "tornado watch," stating that tornadoes may be possible. If you experience a strong thunderstorm and see dark clouds (almost greenish in color) and large hail, these are indicators that a tornado may form. You should go to the basement of your home and stay away from windows. If you do not have a basement, go to a room in the interior of your house. It is also wise to cover your head because tornadoes can whip objects through the air at great speeds.

Standardized Test Practice: Long Reading Passages (Grades 5–6) © 2009 by Michael Priestley, Scholastic Teaching Resources

Blizzards

A blizzard is a dangerous winter storm that combines blowing snow and wind. It usually results in low visibility. That is a measure of the distance you can see clearly. In blizzards, it is possible to look outside your window and see only a wall of white! Meteorologists call this a "white out."

In order to be classified as a blizzard, a storm must have winds greater than 35 miles per hour and visibility less than 1/4 of a mile for at least three hours. This means that you are unable to see more than 1/4 of a mile in front of you. That is the distance around one lap of a running track. On a clear day, you can see for miles and miles, especially if the land is flat. It is interesting to note that a storm doesn't need to occur for a blizzard to form. Strong winds can pick up snow already on the ground to create a ground blizzard with blowing snow.

Forecasters can predict blizzards most of the time. They will put out a "blizzard warning" for the areas where these conditions are anticipated. Blizzards happen most often in the upper Midwest and the Great Plains of the United States. However, they can occur in any place that receives snowfall.

Blizzards are dangerous for several reasons. Driving a car or truck can be hazardous in the slippery snow and ice, and may become impossible since it is difficult to see. The strong wind will make the air temperature feel even colder, so frostbite can develop. Frostbite is damage to the skin from exposure to cold. You should stay indoors during a blizzard. Be sure to have plenty of blankets, water, and a battery-powered radio nearby in case the power goes off.

Questions 1–8: Choose the best answer to each question, or write your answer on the lines provided.

1. **Which sentence best states the main idea of this passage?**

    Ⓐ Our planet can be a calm place, but weather conditions often change rapidly.

    Ⓑ Light snow flurries can become ferocious winter storms.

    Ⓒ It is important to learn about natural disasters so you can be prepared if you face one.

    Ⓓ There are several kinds of natural disasters that may occur in the United States each year, and each one poses significant dangers.

2. **What causes a funnel cloud to form?**

    Ⓐ warm air that circles around

    Ⓑ a gathering of dark clouds

    Ⓒ cold air temperatures

    Ⓓ tropical ocean waters

3. **In the "Tornadoes" section of the passage, the author includes information about tornadoes in North Carolina and South Carolina in order to —**

    Ⓐ show that tornadoes do not always occur in the Midwest.

    Ⓑ give examples of tornadoes that are classified as "weak."

    Ⓒ demonstrate how tornadoes can suck cars and houses into their funnels.

    Ⓓ explain what happens when the sky turns green and hail starts to fall.

4. **The author states that natural disasters create dangerous and destructive conditions. Give two pieces of evidence from the passage that support this statement. (2 points)**

    _____

    _____

    _____

    _____

Standardized Test Practice: Long Reading Passages (Grades 5–6) © 2009 by Michael Priestley, Scholastic Teaching Resources

5. **Which sentence states an opinion?**

Ⓐ A hurricane is a huge storm that forms over warm ocean water.

Ⓑ In order to be classified as a blizzard, a storm must have winds greater than 35 miles per hour and visibility less than 1/4 of a mile for at least three hours.

Ⓒ Radar images give people time to prepare for a coming storm.

Ⓓ Nothing is more frightening than a tornado.

6. **"They will put out a 'blizzard warning' for the areas where these conditions are <u>anticipated</u>."**

What is the meaning of <u>anticipated</u>?

Ⓐ avoided

Ⓑ witnessed

Ⓒ expected

Ⓓ described

7. **In a blizzard, what causes a "white out"?**

Ⓐ heavy rain

Ⓑ blowing snow

Ⓒ large hail

Ⓓ cold temperatures

8. **Using details from the passage, describe four differences between hurricanes and tornadoes. (4 points)**

_____

_____

_____

_____

_____

_____

_____

_____

Name _____ Date _____

Directions: Read "Mystery Paint." Then answer questions 1–8.

Mystery Paint

Amanda, Marcus, and the rest of their sixth-grade classmates sat down on the shiny wood floors in the gymnasium to wait for Mr. Parsons' instructions. It was the third period of the day and time for their physical education class.

"Class, today we are going to practice some soccer drills out on the field," Mr. Parsons explained. "We'll mostly work on ball handling and kicking shots into the goal."

"Oh, I hate playing soccer," Amanda complained. "Can't we practice basketball instead?"

"Amanda, you know we'll start basketball training in a few weeks. We're going to play soccer while the weather is still nice," Mr. Parsons said. "Besides, your kick has really improved. You should go out for the team next year."

Amanda's face brightened at this news, and she quickly joined her classmates who were lined up at the door to go out to the soccer fields. Once outside, the students broke into an easy jog toward the field until, all of a sudden, the group came to a screeching halt.

"Look!" Marcus yelled, pointing toward the track. "What happened to the stadium? It looks . . . angry."

The students turned to see what Marcus was pointing at and gasped all at once.

"Someone painted angry faces all over the walls near the bleachers!" Casey exclaimed.

"I think they look mean. Maybe they'll scare off the visiting team!" Akeem joked.

Mr. Parsons came to the front of the line were the students were gathered. "Oh, dear," he said. "We'll have to report this to Mr. Johnson. I'll let him know after class is dismissed, but right now it's time for soccer."

During lunch, all of the students were buzzing with curiosity about the mysterious graffiti. Possible explanations spread like wildfire around the school.

"I think some kids from Monroe must have done it," Michael proposed. "They're upset because our football team beat them last week."

"I think it must have been some older high school kids," Jessica offered, "because the drawings were really good, even though they were really scary!"

Later in the afternoon during math class, everyone was listening to Mrs. Fields explain how to add and subtract fractions when Amanda noticed something strange. She tapped on Marcus's shoulder in front of her and whispered, "Hey, look at Brian's hands. They have paint all over them!"

"So?" Marcus responded, uninterested. Amanda rolled her eyes at him. "Wait, you don't think that Brian painted the graffiti, do you?" Marcus asked her in disbelief. "He's so quiet! Why would he do that? No way!"

"I think we should follow him to his locker after class. Maybe we'll be able to find some clues to see if it really was him," said Amanda.

When the bell rang, Marcus and Amanda slowly gathered their belongings, waiting for Brian to pack up his books and walk out the door. They quietly followed him down the hall. Brian walked to his locker with his head hung low and his shoulders hunched down the entire way.

"I don't know, Amanda. Brian always looks kind of sad. I don't think he would do it," Marcus said as they approached a group of lockers.

Brian stopped at a locker near the end of the row and began dialing the combination to open his lock. Marcus and Amanda huddled behind a wall and peered around the corner.

Suddenly, Marcus pointed and gasped, "He has cans of paint in there!"

"I told you, Marcus!" Amanda said triumphantly. "What should we do?"

"I guess we should tell Mr. Johnson," Marcus said, shaking his head as they walked toward the principal's office.

The next day during math class, Brian was called to the principal's office. As some of the students oohed and aahed, Brian gathered his books and trudged like a snail toward the door.

Amanda poked Marcus in the back and said, "I bet he's in for it now, and he looks so guilty."

Brian walked to the principal's office and sat down in front of Mr. Johnson, who looked very disappointed. "Brian, can you tell me anything about the graffiti on our stadium walls?" he asked directly.

Brian shuddered and looked down. "I don't know," he mumbled.

"Well, Brian, I noticed that you had paint on your hands yesterday, and you still have some today. I checked your schedule, and you don't have art class until Friday. What is the paint from?"

Suddenly, tears started flowing down Brian's cheeks. "I'm sorry, Mr. Johnson, I like to paint, but I can't join the art club because it's after school, and I have to go right home and baby-sit my little brother. I don't know why I painted those faces, and now I've ruined the stadium!"

Mr. Johnson was quite angry at first, but he began to soften as he realized how miserable Brian was. "Brian, painting graffiti on school property is a very serious matter. We are going to have to call your mother, and you will likely be suspended from school for a few days. And, of course, you are going to have to clean and repaint the walls." Mr. Johnson paused. "But, I must say, those paintings are quite good. Did you have any help with them?"

Brian looked up glumly and said, "No, I did them myself. Drawing and painting are the only things that I can do well."

Mr. Johnson looked at Brian and thought for a moment before making a decision. "Well," he said, "let's go ahead and call your mother to let her know what happened. But first let me tell you that at the faculty meeting the other day, we were discussing the stadium. Some of the teachers suggested that we hire a local artist to paint our school mascot on the stadium wall. How would you feel about participating in that?"

"Really? I mean, you would let me do that?" Brian stammered.

"Yes, but you have to know that this project will be hard work, and you'll be expected to complete the job on time. We can consider it part of your punishment," Mr. Johnson said, trying to hide a smile as he picked up the telephone.

Standardized Test Practice: Long Reading Passages (Grades 5–6) © 2009 by Michael Priestley, Scholastic Teaching Resources

Questions 1–8: Choose the best answer to each question, or write your answer on the lines provided.

1. **Why does Amanda believe that Brian painted the graffiti?**
   - (A) He always looks kind of sad.
   - (B) He is a good artist.
   - (C) He has pictures in his locker.
   - (D) He has paint on his hands.

2. **"I think some kids from Monroe must have done it," Michael proposed."**

   Which word is a synonym for proposed?
   - (A) believed
   - (B) suggested
   - (C) inquired
   - (D) repeated

3. **What can you tell about Brian as Amanda and Marcus follow him down the hall?**
   - (A) He is shy and does not talk to many people.
   - (B) He is disappointed that no one likes his artwork.
   - (C) He is upset because people know he painted the graffiti.
   - (D) He is nervous because he knows that they are following him.

4. **What is the main problem in this passage, and how is it resolved? Use details from the passage in your answer. (2 points)**

   _____

   _____

   _____

   _____

Standardized Test Practice: Long Reading Passages (Grades 5–6) © 2009 by Michael Priestley, Scholastic Teaching Resources

5. "Brian gathered his books and trudged like a snail toward the door."

   What does the simile in this sentence suggest about Brian?

   (A) He sat on the floor.

   (B) He looks like a snail.

   (C) He has a hard shell.

   (D) He moved very slowly.

6. Why can't Brian join the art club?

   (A) He has to baby-sit after school.

   (B) He does not have enough money.

   (C) He has no talent for painting.

   (D) He does not have many friends.

7. How does Brian probably feel at the end of the passage?

   (A) sad

   (B) worried

   (C) hopeful

   (D) confident

8. What kind of passage is this?

   (A) informational article

   (B) news report

   (C) realistic fiction

   (D) folk tale

Standardized Test Practice: Long Reading Passages (Grades 5–6) © 2009 by Michael Priestley, Scholastic Teaching Resources

Name _____   Date _____

Standardized Test Practice: Long Reading Passages (Grades 5–6) © 2009 by Michael Priestley, Scholastic Teaching Resources

Directions: Read "Missing Birds." Then answer questions 1–9.

Missing Birds

About 500 years ago, there were at least a dozen species of birds living in different parts of the world that are no longer with us today. They are now extinct. How did these bird species become extinct? The main reason is people.

The human population has grown and spread to every corner of the world. This growth has affected other species in many ways. For example, in many places, people use wood to build houses. When people move into an area, they cut down trees for wood. If people cut down all the trees in a forest, then creatures that live in the trees will not survive. They have lost their natural habitat.

People have contributed to the disappearance of many kinds of birds. Looking at some of these cases may help us better understand what happened to these birds. Perhaps it will also help us prevent this kind of loss in the future.

Dodos

The most famous extinct bird is probably the dodo. You may remember that the dodo was a character in the story of Alice in Wonderland. But the man who wrote *Alice's Adventures in Wonderland* in the 1800s had never seen a dodo. They were already extinct.

In the late 1500s, dodos lived in only one place: the island of Mauritius. This small island lies off the coast of Madagascar, near Africa. When Dutch sailors landed on this island in 1598, they encountered the dodo. No Europeans had ever seen a dodo before that.

An adult dodo weighed as much as 50 pounds. It had short legs and short, stubby wings. But it could not fly. It also had an oddly shaped beak. Some scientists think that the dodo used its beak to catch and eat fish, or to open up fruit.

The island of Mauritius was an ideal place for the dodo. It had lots of low-lying fruit and plenty of fish to satisfy the dodo's appetite. Also, there were no predators on the island to threaten the dodo. This was a good thing because the dodo could not fly or run fast enough to escape from any predators.

When sailors landed on the island, they hunted the dodo for food. Then they cut down much of the forest on the island. So the dodo's home and food supply were in danger. Finally, sailors brought their own pets and other animals—cats, monkeys, rats, and pigs—to the island. These animals fed on dodo eggs. They destroyed the dodos' nests. Within about 80 years, the entire dodo population was completely wiped out.

Other Island Birds

Not far from Mauritius are two other small islands called Rodrigues and Reunion. A bird called the solitaire lived on both of these islands, but nowhere else in the world. French sailors first saw these birds around 1690. The sailors landed on the islands looking for food and water.

Solitaires were gray or brown birds about 3 feet tall (90 cm), and they were flightless. Solitaires were closely related to the dodo, and their fate was the same. Sailors and their pets ate the solitaire eggs and hunted the birds. By about 1761, the solitaires were gone.

The same thing happened to the great auk. This bird lived mainly on islands in the North Atlantic Ocean. It was a large bird that looked like a penguin. But, like the dodo and the solitaire, it could not fly. Sailors and explorers who crossed the Atlantic Ocean often stopped on the islands to gather food and water. The great auk and its eggs fed many sailors until the bird became extinct around 1844.

Passenger Pigeons

At one time, the most abundant bird species in North America was the passenger pigeon. Scientists think there were 3 to 5 billion of these birds living in North America when Europeans first arrived.

Passenger pigeons traveled in huge flocks, and they migrated every spring and fall. The largest flocks of birds lived mainly in the Midwest and in eastern Canada. Every winter they migrated to Texas, Louisiana, Georgia, Florida, and other areas in the southern United States. The flocks of migrating birds were so large that they sometimes stretched a mile wide and 300 miles long. The skies would be dark with birds for hours at a time as the flocks traveled by.

Standardized Test Practice: Long Reading Passages (Grades 5–6) © 2009 by Michael Priestley, Scholastic Teaching Resources

Passenger pigeons were about 16 inches tall with long wings and a long, thin tail. Their feathers were mostly gray or grayish-blue with a reddish tinge on the breast. In flight, these birds could reach speeds of 60 or 70 miles per hour.

Unfortunately, passenger pigeons roosted together in large numbers. Sometimes millions of birds would live in a forest. Hundreds of birds might live in a single tree. The birds fed mainly on nuts, acorns, seeds, and berries. When the food supply in one forest ran out, the flock moved on to another forest.

By the mid-1800s, people in America were cutting down forests at a rapid pace and turning them into farmlands. They were also hunting and trapping passenger pigeons for food. Since the pigeons roosted together in large numbers, they were easy to catch. In some places, hunters and trappers were catching 50,000 birds a day.

By the 1890s, the passenger pigeons were almost gone. Without large forests to roost in, the birds could not survive. The last known passenger pigeon was captured and placed in the Cincinnati Zoo. It was named Martha, after Martha Washington. This bird died at 1:00 PM on September 1, 1914. The passenger pigeon may be the only species for whom we know the exact moment it became extinct.

Ivory-Billed Woodpeckers

There are several other species of birds that are believed to be extinct. These include the Carolina parakeet and the Bachman's warbler. But one notorious bird is the ivory-billed woodpecker. This was a very large species of woodpecker (18 to 20 inches long) with a straight, chisel-shaped beak. It was glossy black with white markings on each side and a red crest (for the male). The noise it made was often compared to the tooting sound of a tin horn.

The ivory-billed woodpecker was once fairly common in southern hardwood forests. But many of those forests were cut down to make room for people. By about 1952, the ivory-bill was thought to have disappeared.

In 2004, birdwatchers and scientists heard some exciting news. Two men canoeing through a swamp in Arkansas heard a tooting sound coming from the branches of a tree. When they looked closely, they spotted an ivory-billed woodpecker—or at least they thought they did. The sighting immediately became big news all over the country. Many bird experts traveled to Arkansas to see the bird. But no one ever saw it again. The bird experts could not confirm that an ivory-billed woodpecker lived in the swamp, and the reported sighting has still not been verified.

As you can tell from these short reports, several species of birds have become extinct in the last few centuries. In every case, people have contributed to their demise, either by destroying habitats or by hunting the birds themselves. Scientists who have studied the extinction of the dodo, the solitaire, and the passenger pigeon hope that they will serve as lessons for modern-day society. Sailors and settlers in the 1600s may not have understood the results of their actions. But today, we understand a lot more about the effects of human activities on the environment. Perhaps our knowledge can help stop future extinctions.

Questions 1–9: Choose the best answer to each question, or write your answer on the lines provided.

1. The author's main purpose in this passage is to —

Ⓐ persuade readers to help save the dodo and the passenger pigeon.

Ⓑ entertain readers with a story about a flightless bird.

Ⓒ explain why sailors should not be allowed to land on unpopulated islands.

Ⓓ give information about certain birds that became extinct.

2. "When Dutch sailors landed on this island in 1598, they **encountered** the dodo."

Which word is a synonym for encountered?

Ⓐ met

Ⓑ remembered

Ⓒ cured

Ⓓ disliked

3. How did cats, rats, and pigs affect the dodo?

Ⓐ They ate all the food on the island.

Ⓑ They hid the dodos' nests.

Ⓒ They ate the dodos' eggs.

Ⓓ They brought more sailors to the island.

Standardized Test Practice: Long Reading Passages (Grades 5–6) © 2009 by Michael Priestley, Scholastic Teaching Resources

Standardized Test Practice: Long Reading Passages (Grades 5–6) © 2009 by Michael Priestley, Scholastic Teaching Resources

Name _____ Date _____

4. Describe four ways the dodo, the solitaire, and the great auk were similar. (4 points)

_____

_____

_____

_____

_____

_____

_____

5. Which information belongs in the empty oval?

(A) no predators

(B) lived in nests

(C) stubby wings

(D) ate fish

Use this web to answer question 5.

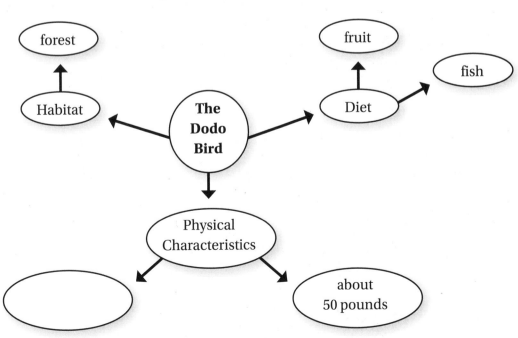

6. **Which of these is an example of habitat loss?**

   Ⓐ New animals come to an area and eat all of the food supply.

   Ⓑ People remove sand and tall grasses along the coast to build houses.

   Ⓒ Fishermen catch hundreds of fish from the ocean each day.

   Ⓓ A large animal in the forest eats smaller animals as part of its diet.

7. **Why were passenger pigeons easy to hunt and trap?**

   Ⓐ They had grayish-blue feathers.

   Ⓑ They roosted together in large numbers.

   Ⓒ They were 16 inches tall.

   Ⓓ They could fly 60 to 70 miles per hour.

8. **How were the passenger pigeon and the ivory-billed woodpecker alike, and how were they different? (2 points)**

   _____

   _____

   _____

   _____

9. **What evidence made people think that the ivory-billed woodpecker was not extinct?**

   Ⓐ Two men said they saw one in 2004.

   Ⓑ It made a tooting sound like a tin horn.

   Ⓒ This bird disappeared around 1952.

   Ⓓ It was once common in southern forests.

Standardized Test Practice: Long Reading Passages (Grades 5–6) © 2009 by Michael Priestley, Scholastic Teaching Resources

Name _____   Date _____

Directions: Read Document A: "Harnessing Wind Power" and
Document B: "Don't Spoil the Seashore." Then answer questions 1–8.

Document A: Harnessing Wind Power

Wind is a valuable source of energy with
great potential. The energy created by wind can
be turned into electricity to light our houses
and power our computers. Wind is a renewable
natural resource—one that can't be used up.
It will always be windy somewhere in the
world. Unlike fossil fuels, such as oil and coal,
wind energy does not cause pollution. To get
energy from fossil fuels, we have to burn them.
Burning oil and coal sends gases into the air,
causing pollution. Also, fossil fuels can run out.
Someday the supply of fossil fuels will be gone.

People have been using the wind for centuries. At least 2,000 years
ago, people discovered how to capture wind to do work. They made sails
for their boats. They built windmills to draw water for their farms. People
in the Netherlands built windmills to pump water and saw wood as early
as the 1400s. Windmills have been used to pump water and mill grain
since the late 1780s in the United States.

The idea behind wind power is simple. The windmills capture
breezes, which cause their blades to spin. This spinning motion turns the
wind into energy. Old windmills were usually made from wood and had
several blades. Today's modern windmills are called wind turbines. These
turbines usually have three blades and may be more than 300 feet tall.
They are usually made from aluminum or steel.

Thirty-three states now generate energy from wind turbines.
California is the biggest producer of wind energy in the United States. It
has thousands of turbines in use.

When deciding where to build a wind farm (or wind park), it is
important to measure how strong the wind is and its direction. Some
places just don't get enough wind to support a wind farm. One place
where wind farms can be successful is in or near the ocean along a
windy coast.

One new project in the works is the Cape Wind project on Cape Cod, Massachusetts. Cape Cod is a good place for a wind farm because it is a peninsula. It is surrounded by water on three sides. Engineers plan to put 130 wind turbines about six miles off the coast of Cape Cod in a body of water called Nantucket Sound. This wind farm will produce 75 percent of Cape Cod's energy. It will make use of a renewable energy source and reduce pollution. It will also help the United States rely less on fossil fuels. The Cape Wind project is a terrific idea.

Document B: Don't Spoil the Seashore

Climate change is a large concern for the United States. We know that we need to reduce global warming by conserving fuel and finding new energy sources. One of the most valuable resources we can use is wind power. Using wind as a form of energy can reduce our use of fossil fuels, such as oil and coal. These fuels pollute the environment and are expensive to buy.

However, I also believe in building large wind farms in the right places. As a life-long resident of Cape Cod, Massachusetts, I really enjoy the dune-covered beaches. I like digging for clams in the muddy sand along the shore. I cannot imagine looking out at the ocean and having my view marred by more than 100 steel wind turbines sticking up 400 feet into the air. The Cape Cod coast is not an appropriate place to put a wind farm. It would ruin the natural beauty of our coast.

A wind farm on Cape Cod may also affect local fishermen. These fishermen earn money catching cod, haddock, and other fish. A wind farm would surely reduce the number of fish and other marine life in Nantucket Sound. How will these fishermen earn enough income to support their families if they can no longer fish here?

Also, these 130 huge steel turbines will be dangerous. How can fishermen navigate their boats around them? Plus, birds that live on Cape Cod may fly into the turbines. This would mean instant death. In Altamont Pass, California, the wind turbines slaughter more than 1,000 birds each year. Do we really want to bring this kind of danger to Cape Cod?

Standardized Test Practice: Long Reading Passages (Grades 5–6) © 2009 by Michael Priestley, Scholastic Teaching Resources

Some people argue that the turbines won't be much of a blot on the horizon. I wonder if these people have ever watched the pods of humpback whales and the harbor seals that make their home in Nantucket Sound. Imagine what 130 ugly steel towers would do to that scene. How would these people feel if 130 turbines were built in their backyard?

I understand the need for finding alternative sources of energy. I understand that wind energy is cost-effective and clean. But I also feel the need to keep our shoreline as beautiful and as natural as possible. There has to be a better place for this wind farm. I am urging you to study other possibilities.

Questions 1–8: Choose the best answer to each question, or write your answer on the lines provided.

1. **In Document A, what is the main topic of the first paragraph?**

   Ⓐ the benefits of renewable resources

   Ⓑ why fossil fuels need to burn

   Ⓒ our need for electricity

   Ⓓ the importance of wind, oil, and coal

2. **In Document A, what is the main idea of the second paragraph?**

   Ⓐ Windmills are used in the United States and in the Netherlands.

   Ⓑ The spinning blades on a windmill create wind energy.

   Ⓒ People have been using wind power for thousands of years.

   Ⓓ Some windmills are built to saw wood.

3. **Which sentence from Document A states an opinion?**

   Ⓐ Old windmills were usually made from wood and had several blades.

   Ⓑ Thirty-three states now generate energy from wind turbines.

   Ⓒ California is the biggest producer of wind energy in the United States.

   Ⓓ The Cape Wind project is a terrific idea.

4. In Document A, what evidence does the author give to show the benefits of the Cape Wind project?

(A) Cape Cod is a good place for a wind farm because it is a peninsula.

(B) The turbines will supply Cape Cod with 75 percent of its electricity.

(C) Engineers will build 130 turbines to collect wind energy.

(D) Wind turbines will be placed in the Nantucket Sound about six miles from the coast.

5. Describe two ways wind energy was used in the past. Use specific details from the passage in your answer. (2 points)

_____

_____

_____

_____

6. Read this sentence from Document B.

I cannot imagine looking out at the ocean and having my view <u>marred</u> by more than 100 steel wind turbines sticking up 400 feet into the air.

What is the meaning of <u>marred</u>?

(A) forced

(B) outlined

(C) spoiled

(D) controlled

Standardized Test Practice: Long Reading Passages (Grades 5–6) © 2009 by Michael Priestley, Scholastic Teaching Resources

7. **In Document B, the author's main purpose is to —**

Ⓐ inform Americans about pollution caused by fossil fuels.

Ⓑ persuade experts to put the Cape Cod wind farm somewhere else.

Ⓒ convince Americans that wind energy is important.

Ⓓ describe the natural beauty of Cape Cod and its surrounding waters.

8. **With which sentence would the authors of both documents most likely agree?**

Ⓐ Wind turbines are noisy and should not be placed anywhere near people's homes.

Ⓑ Fishermen will no longer be able to fish off the coast because of the Cape Cod wind farm.

Ⓒ Even if some birds are killed during the process, we need to use wind energy.

Ⓓ Using fossil fuels is expensive, and it causes pollution.

Name _____ Date _____

Directions: Read "The Walrus and the Carpenter." Then answer questions 1–6.

The Walrus and the Carpenter

The sun was shining on the sea,
    Shining with all his might:
He did his very best to make
    The billows smooth and bright—
And this was odd, because it was   5
    The middle of the night.

The moon was shining sulkily,
    Because she thought the sun
Had got no business to be there
    After the day was done—   10
"It's very rude of him," she said,
    "To come and spoil the fun."

The sea was wet as wet could be,
    The sands were dry as dry.
You could not see a cloud, because   15
    No cloud was in the sky:
No birds were flying overhead—
    There were no birds to fly.

Standardized Test Practice: Long Reading Passages (Grades 5–6) © 2009 by Michael Priestley, Scholastic Teaching Resources

The Walrus and the Carpenter
 Were walking close at hand;   20
They wept like anything to see
 Such quantities of sand:
"If this were only cleared away,"
 They said, "it *would* be grand!"

"If seven maids with seven mops   25
 Swept it for half a year,
Do you suppose," the Walrus said,
 "That they could get it clear?"
"I doubt it," said the Carpenter,
 And shed a bitter tear.   30

"O Oysters, come and walk with us!"
 The Walrus did beseech.
"A pleasant walk, a pleasant talk,
 Along the briny beach:
We cannot do with more than four,   35
 To give a hand to each."

The eldest Oyster looked at him,
 But never a word he said:
The eldest Oyster winked his eye,
 And shook his heavy head—   40
Meaning to say he did not choose
 To leave the oyster-bed.

But four young Oysters hurried up,
 All eager for the treat:
Their coats were brushed, their faces washed, 45
 Their shoes were clean and neat—
And this was odd, because, you know,
 They hadn't any feet.

Standardized Test Practice: Long Reading Passages (Grades 5–6) © 2009 by Michael Priestley, Scholastic Teaching Resources

Four other Oysters followed them,
    And yet another four;   50
And thick and fast they came at last,
    And more, and more, and more—
All hopping through the frothy waves,
    And scrambling to the shore.

The Walrus and the Carpenter   55
    Walked on a mile or so,
And then they rested on a rock
    Conveniently low:
And all the little Oysters stood
    And waited in a row.   60

"The time has come," the Walrus said,
    "To talk of many things:
Of shoes—and ships—and sealing-wax—
    Of cabbages—and kings—
And why the sea is boiling hot—   65
    And whether pigs have wings."

"But wait a bit," the Oysters cried,
    "Before we have our chat;
For some of us are out of breath,
    And all of us are fat!"   70
"No hurry!" said the Carpenter.
    They thanked him much for that.

"A loaf of bread," the Walrus said,
    "Is what we chiefly need:
Pepper and vinegar besides   75
    Are very good indeed—
Now if you're ready, Oysters dear,
    We can begin to feed."

Standardized Test Practice: Long Reading Passages (Grades 5–6) © 2009 by Michael Priestley, Scholastic Teaching Resources

"But not on us!" the Oysters cried,
    Turning a little blue.   80
"After such kindness, that would be
    A dismal thing to do!"
"The night is fine," the Walrus said.
    "Do you admire the view?

"It was so kind of you to come!   85
    And you are very nice!"
The Carpenter said nothing but
    "Cut us another slice:
I wish you were not quite so deaf—
    I've had to ask you twice!"   90

"It seems a shame," the Walrus said,
    "To play them such a trick,
After we've brought them out so far,
    And made them trot so quick!"
The Carpenter said nothing but   95
    "The butter's spread too thick!"

"I weep for you," the Walrus said:
    "I deeply sympathize."
With sobs and tears he sorted out
    Those of the largest size,   100
Holding his pocket-handkerchief
    Before his streaming eyes.

"O Oysters," said the Carpenter,
    "You've had a pleasant run!
Shall we be trotting home again?"   105
    But answer came there none—
And this was scarcely odd, because
    They'd eaten every one."

—*Lewis Carroll (1832–1898)*

Standardized Test Practice: Long Reading Passages (Grades 5–6) © 2009 by Michael Priestley, Scholastic Teaching Resources

Questions 1–6: Choose the best answer to each question, or write your answer on the lines provided.

1. **What unusual thing happens at the beginning of the poem?**

   Ⓐ Rain falls on the sea.

   Ⓑ The sun shines at night.

   Ⓒ A bird flies across the sky.

   Ⓓ The sun speaks to the moon.

2. **Why did the Walrus and the Carpenter start weeping as they walked?**

   Ⓐ There was too much sand on the beach.

   Ⓑ They were hungry and had nothing to eat.

   Ⓒ There weren't any clouds in the sky.

   Ⓓ They saw seven maids working very hard.

3. **Explain why the young Oysters came out of the water. (2 points)**

   _____

   _____

   _____

   _____

Standardized Test Practice: Long Reading Passages (Grades 5–6) © 2009 by Michael Priestley, Scholastic Teaching Resources

4. How did the Oysters feel when the Walrus said, "We can begin to feed" (line 78)?

(A) excited

(B) ashamed

(C) worried

(D) pleased

5. What "trick" did the Walrus and the Carpenter play on the Oysters? Explain. (2 points)

_____

_____

_____

_____

6. Which word best describes the mood of this poem?

(A) frightening

(B) sad

(C) homesick

(D) silly

Name _____   Date _____

Directions: Read "Baseball Magic." Then answer questions 1–8.

Baseball Magic

On the last day of school in June of that year, Dad said to me, "If you don't bite your nails for the whole summer, I'll take you to a Red Sox game."

I was 10 years old, and even I could see that my nails looked pretty bad. Nothing my parents had tried so far had gotten me to stop biting them. Mom and Dad knew I liked baseball because my friends and I would play 'til it got too dark to see the ball. But going to a Sox game—wow! None of my friends had been to a professional game, although a bunch of us had been listening to games on the radio for about a year. So I guess Dad really knew how to motivate me.

The first two days of not biting my nails were the toughest, but after that it was pretty easy. By August, it was clear that my nail-biting habit was over. True to his word, Dad bought us two tickets for a Red Sox game— *and* they were playing the Yankees! The Boston Red Sox and the New York Yankees were two of the best teams (and biggest rivals) in the American League in the 1950s.

When the big night arrived, we stood on Yawkey Way outside Fenway Park with thousands of people, mostly grownups. As the crowd pressed toward the ticket takers, all I could see was elbows and backs. I was afraid I'd lose my dad and never find him again, so I grabbed the bottom of his jacket. After they took our tickets, we were funneled through a huge, dark hallway that didn't smell very good. The crowd packed together even closer. Fortunately, I still had a grip on Dad's jacket. We shuffled forward in the enormous, smelly hallway, which gradually started sloping upward. After a few more minutes of pushing forward in the dark, we were suddenly surrounded by blazing stadium lights and faced with an amazing scene. Out in the open grandstand, we found cool, fresh air. A huge crowd roared around a brilliant, glowing green field, so much greener than our own lawn at home.

Standardized Test Practice: Long Reading Passages (Grades 5–6) © 2009 by Michael Priestley, Scholastic Teaching Resources

Dad had managed to get us seats behind home plate, about halfway up the grandstand. He pointed out the microphone hanging on a long wire from the press box above us. "That's so the people who are listening to the game on the radio can hear the crowd," he explained.

"You mean, I could say hi to Mom and she'd hear me on the radio?" I asked.

"Well, you could, but how would she know it was you?" said Dad with a laugh.

The players were warming up on the sidelines. About 10 yards separated me from guys who, until now, I'd seen only in the newspaper. I saw Ted Williams, Jackie Jensen, and even my favorite, Jimmy Piersall.

The Yankee pitchers were taking turns doing practice throws with catcher Yogi Berra. Then Yogi turned his back to one pitcher and put his glove behind him with the palm facing out. Thwack! The ball slammed into the center of Yogi's glove, and he calmly turned around and threw it back.

Dad told me they were trying to intimidate the Sox with the Yankees' pitching prowess. I don't know if the Sox were impressed, but I certainly was. As a 10-year-old budding shortstop, I couldn't imagine being able to hit pitches like that.

Foul balls from the batters flew up into a big net behind home plate that emptied out onto the field. When a ball went foul, the crowd let out a long, rising "whoo-o-o-op" that didn't end 'til the ball rolled down the net and plopped into the batboy's waiting glove.

It was a great game. Mickey Mantle hit the longest home run I have ever seen. It almost struck the clock above the bleachers. Although the Yanks led for most of the game, the Sox finally turned it around and won in the end. As we walked out of the stadium late on that crisp September night, I knew I had just become a baseball fan for life.

Standardized Test Practice: Long Reading Passages (Grades 5–6) © 2009 by Michael Priestley, Scholastic Teaching Resources

Questions 1–8: Choose the best answer to each question, or write your answer on the lines provided.

1. **Why did the father take his son to the ball game?**

    (A) so the boy could learn how to play baseball

    (B) because his son loved baseball so much

    (C) to fulfill a promise he had made

    (D) to impress his son's friends

2. **"Dad told me they were trying to intimidate the Sox with the Yankees' pitching prowess."**

    What does the word prowess mean in this sentence?

    (A) skill

    (B) habit

    (C) reputation

    (D) angle

3. **Which phrase best describes the narrator of this story?**

    (A) a father who has done something he regrets

    (B) a young boy experiencing a baseball game

    (C) an older man looking back on a boyhood event

    (D) a person outside the story

Standardized Test Practice: Long Reading Passages (Grades 5–6) © 2009 by Michael Priestley, Scholastic Teaching Resources

4. **What is the most likely reason the boy had seen baseball players only in the newspaper?**

Ⓐ Baseball wasn't a popular sport yet.

Ⓑ Baseball wasn't regularly broadcast on TV at the time.

Ⓒ His parents wouldn't let him watch games on TV.

Ⓓ He couldn't stop biting his nails.

5. **The narrator says, "So I guess Dad really knew how to motivate me." Explain what the narrator meant by this. (2 points)**

_____

_____

_____

_____

6. **What happened last in this story?**

Ⓐ The batboy caught a foul ball.

Ⓑ Mickey Mantle hit a long home run.

Ⓒ Yogi Berra caught a ball behind his back.

Ⓓ The narrator and his father left the stadium.

7. **Which word best describes the mood of this passage?**

Ⓐ hopeful

Ⓑ disappointed

Ⓒ nervous

Ⓓ exciting

8. **In a few sentences, summarize the narrator's impressions of the stadium on the night of the game. Include at least four details from the passage to support your answer. (4 points)**

_____

_____

_____

_____

_____

_____

_____

_____

Standardized Test Practice: Long Reading Passages (Grades 5–6) © 2009 by Michael Priestley, Scholastic Teaching Resources

Name _____ Date _____

Directions: Read Selection 1: "The Brotherhood of the Rails" and Selection 2: "Steam Train Maury, King of the Hobos." Then answer questions 1–10.

SELECTION 1: The Brotherhood of the Rails

At certain times in America's past, many men traveled around the country as hobos. They were homeless men who didn't stay in one place too long. Most people thought of hobos as carefree tramps or troublemakers. They thought hobos traveled the country avoiding work and causing problems. The truth is rather different.

Actually, hoboing started right after the Civil War in the 1860s. Many of the original hobos were ex-soldiers. They had come to prefer army living to a more settled life. They slept in the open, cooked over a campfire, and walked everywhere.

As the railroads grew, wandering on foot turned into hopping freight trains. Riding in an open boxcar was a fast and free way to get around. It was also uncomfortable, dangerous, and illegal. But the railroad police often turned a blind eye.

After World War I ended in 1918, more ex-soldiers became hobos. Many of these men were still wandering when the Great Depression hit in the 1930s. Thousands of people lost their jobs. At that time, the ranks of hobos swelled with thousands of men and even whole families leaving home in search of work. Catching freight trains, sleeping under the stars, and doing chores in exchange for a meal seemed better than staying home doing nothing. The lure of adventure added spice to this hard life.

Never a Bum

One thing hobos insisted on was working for a living. In fact, that stick over the shoulder was usually a hoe. Every farm and garden needed hoeing to keep weeds down. A traveling "hoe-boy" (which soon became "hobo") was often welcome on a farm. Farmers always had work to do.

Hobos helped with the harvest and did odd jobs in towns and cities across the country. If they couldn't find work, they could ask their brother hobos where to find some. Like members of a family, hobos helped each other in many ways. Knowing where to locate a generous family or which policemen would run them out of town was a matter of survival.

When work was scarce, each hobo fell back on a trade or craft. Their bundles held their working tools, known as their "traveling trade." Tools might include needles and thread, leather, pliers, and deerskin. Many hobos hunted, fished, and gathered wild greens. At night in the hobo camp, or "jungle," a big pot would go on the fire. Whatever food people had scraped together would go into the pot. Then everyone ate a hot meal.

Rules of the Road

A hobo shared what he had because he never knew when he himself would need help. This is part of the Hobo Code, a list of rules agreed on at the annual hobo convention in Chicago in 1894. According to the code, a hobo should always act like a gentleman. He should respect local lawmen and leave no garbage in camp. Other rules included staying as clean as possible, causing no problems with a train or its crew, and even acting like an extra crew member when needed.

It may seem odd that these free spirits had meetings and rules. In fact, meetings of hobos are still going on. These days they meet in a hall in the small town of Britt, Iowa. They elect a king and queen of the hobos. They swap stories and catch up on the news about old friends. No matter how much hobos like to get together, though, the first rule of the Hobo Code may be the most important: "Decide your own life. Don't let another person run or rule you."

Standardized Test Practice: Long Reading Passages (Grades 5–6) © 2009 by Michael Priestley, Scholastic Teaching Resources

SELECTION 2:
Steam Train Maury, King of the Hobos

Maurice W. Graham was 14 when he left home. It was 1931. His mother had died the year before, and he was living with his father in Toledo, Ohio. Maury wanted to go back to Idaho where he'd spent some of his early years. The only way to get there was to sneak onto a freight train.

He was in good company. Not only were lots of "professional" hobos traveling by train in those days, but a large number of them were teenagers. During the Depression, thousands of jobless people rode the rails. The railroad owners called it trespassing, and catching a ride on a train certainly was dangerous. Hundreds of people were killed or injured every year while riding trains illegally.

Naturally, Maury's father didn't approve of his plan. But he did not stop his son. Eventually, the boy came back to Ohio, but he spent the next few summers working in the West. He always got there in a boxcar.

Over the next few years, Maury lived the life of a hobo most of the time. He spent many nights sitting by a flickering campfire in a hobo camp, which was often called a "jungle." He listened to a lot of the old-time hobos. They were in their sixties and seventies, and Maury learned a lot from them about the history of hobos.

He found that few of them traveled because they had to. Many hobos traveled because they wanted to see the world and share their experiences with others. When they weren't riding trains, they lived in the jungle camps. These camps were often located next to rivers or creeks so the men could cook and wash clothes. And many of the hobos got pretty good at living off the land. They knew the wild foods they could eat, and they knew where to find them.

Later in the '30s, Maurice got married and settled down in Toledo. He worked as a cement mason and later opened a school for masons. He also served in World War II as a medical technician.

By 1971, Maury had a bad hip that made it hard for him to work much. His wife, Wanda, got annoyed with him for sitting around the house while she worked and took care of their daughters. So one day he hopped a freight train as it left Toledo. He thought the trip might give his wife a break and bring back old memories. He figured he'd be back in a few weeks.

While he was on the road, Maury helped establish the Hobo Museum in Britt, Iowa. In the following years, he was voted King of the Hobos—in 1973, 1975, 1976, 1978, and 1981—more often than anyone else. His hobo "family" loved him, but he seemed to have forgotten his real family.

In 1981, after not even telling Wanda where he was for 10 years, he went home. She eventually took him back. From that point on, Steam Train Maury traveled only by car and with his wife. They often went to hobo events, and he visited old friends who were now in hospitals or prisons. In 1990, he and Robert J. Hemming wrote a book called *Tales of the Iron Road: My Life as King of the Hobos.*

In November 2006, after a long lifetime of sharing hobo history with the world, Steam Train Maury died. In hobo terms, that final trip is known as "taking the westbound."

Standardized Test Practice: Long Reading Passages (Grades 5–6) © 2009 by Michael Priestley, Scholastic Teaching Resources

Questions 1–10: Choose the best answer to each question, or write your answer on the lines provided.

1. In "The Brotherhood of the Rails," the author's main purpose is to —

   Ⓐ convince readers that a hobo's life was carefree.

   Ⓑ tell the true history of hobos.

   Ⓒ warn readers about the dangers of a hobo's life.

   Ⓓ explain how to survive as a hobo.

2. List four factual details about hobo life that are mentioned in both selections. **(4 points)**

   _____

   _____

   _____

   _____

   _____

   _____

   _____

   _____

3. Before the Depression, most of the men who became hobos were —

   Ⓐ farmers.

   Ⓑ writers.

   Ⓒ railroad police.

   Ⓓ ex-soldiers.

Standardized Test Practice: Long Reading Passages (Grades 5–6) © 2009 by Michael Priestley, Scholastic Teaching Resources

4. "Riding in an open boxcar was a fast and free way to get around. It was also uncomfortable, dangerous, and illegal. But railroad police often <u>turned a blind eye</u>."

   What does the phrase <u>turned a blind eye</u> most likely mean?

   Ⓐ refused to help

   Ⓑ had bad eyesight

   Ⓒ moved away from

   Ⓓ pretended not to see

5. **Why did hobos often share food and information with other hobos?**

   Ⓐ They expected the same treatment if they were in need.

   Ⓑ Most hobos did not eat much and could not read.

   Ⓒ There was always plenty of food and information to go around.

   Ⓓ At conventions, hobos signed a pledge to share what they had.

6. **In Selection 2, the author's main purpose is to —**

   Ⓐ compare the lives of teenaged hobos and professional hobos.

   Ⓑ summarize the life of a well-known hobo.

   Ⓒ explain that being a hobo can affect a marriage.

   Ⓓ describe a trip to the Hobo Museum in Iowa.

7. "This is part of the Hobo Code, a list of rules agreed on at the <u>annual</u> hobo convention held in Chicago in 1894."

   What does the word <u>annual</u> mean in the sentence above?

   Ⓐ against the law

   Ⓑ crowded

   Ⓒ once a year

   Ⓓ popular

8. **What did Maury Graham do before he got married?**

   (A) He rode the rails from Ohio to Idaho.

   (B) He worked in Ohio as a cement mason.

   (C) He wrote a book about living as a hobo.

   (D) He got elected King of the Hobos.

9. **What did Steam Train Maury do after returning to his wife Wanda in 1981?**

   Use details from the selection to support your answer. (2 points)

   _____

   _____

   _____

   _____

10. **Selection 1 says that one of the hobo rules was "staying as clean as possible."**

   Which detail from Selection 2 supports this statement?

   (A) "Many hobos traveled because they wanted to see the world and share their experiences with others."

   (B) "He found that few of them traveled because they had to."

   (C) "And many of the hobos got pretty good at living off the land."

   (D) "These camps were often located next to rivers or creeks so the men could cook and wash clothes."

Name _____ Date _____

Directions: Read "A Very Big Snake." Then answer questions 1–10.

A Very Big Snake

When biologist Dr. Jesus Rivas goes looking for South America's largest snake, he takes off his shoes and socks. Using his bare feet is the best way to feel for the anaconda's texture and shape as it lurks in swampy jungles or rivers with shallow water. Rivas must know what he's doing. He has caught and measured more than 900 of the giant reptiles.

Anacondas may grow 25 to 30 feet long and weigh up to 500 pounds. The anaconda is usually considered the world's biggest snake. Its chief rival for the title is the reticulated python of Asia. The longest python ever captured measured 33 feet, which is a bit longer than the largest anaconda ever found. But the anaconda wins the prize for biggest circumference. Its long body can be as big around as an adult man.

Some snakes kill by poisoning their victims with their fangs. Constrictors kill by wrapping their bodies around prey and squeezing it. Both anacondas and pythons are constrictors. Anacondas use their teeth to hold onto prey and keep it from escaping until they can swallow it.

The anaconda hunts mostly by lying in a river or shallow pool. Its head barely breaks the surface—just enough so it can breathe. There it waits for birds, deer, rodents, jaguars, and even other snakes to come for a drink. Fish and reptiles are completely acceptable food, too. The anaconda climbs as well as it swims, and so it sometimes hides in trees. Since this big snake can't move very fast, it stays extremely still. It relies on surprise to get its dinner. It sometimes drags prey under water to drown it and then swallows the animal whole.

Standardized Test Practice: Long Reading Passages (Grades 5–6) © 2009 by Michael Priestley, Scholastic Teaching Resources

Big Dinner

The snake's mouth is hinged to swing wide open, like a gate. Its jaws are joined by stretchy ligaments rather than bone. A snake's body is mostly one long ribcage. Snakes have no breastbone, though, so the ribs are not joined on the belly side. This lets a large meal slide through the digestive tract without getting stuck anywhere.

The anaconda has greenish brown scales with black spots. These scales cover a stretchy skin. When the anaconda's body is swollen with a meal, the scales spread out so they look like widely spaced spots on the stretched-out skin. Like many other snakes, the anaconda can digest bone, eggshells, and teeth. But the process may take a while. If you came upon an anaconda right after it swallowed a large meal, you might have to wait a few weeks to see it move.

Smelling With Its Tongue

An anaconda's nostrils are on top of the head, so it can breathe without bringing its head totally out of the water. But snakes don't smell with their nostrils. All snakes use their tongues to smell. That's why they always flick their tongues out: they are sampling the air in their environment. A special organ in the roof of the mouth acts like the inside of a person's nose. The snake touches its tongue to this sense organ so the brain can read the smell signals.

Snakes are much more common in warm places than in cold because they cannot keep themselves warm. Rivers such as the Orinoco and the Amazon in steamy Venezuela and Brazil are ideal homes for anacondas and other large snakes.

Like other snakes, the anaconda cannot hear. But it does have an "ear" bone near the jaw that picks up vibrations in the ground. Deafness might be a problem for a smaller animal, but not many animals bother a snake this big.

Standardized Test Practice: Long Reading Passages (Grades 5–6) © 2009 by Michael Priestley, Scholastic Teaching Resources

Name _____ Date _____

Snake Wrestler

Anacondas are as beautiful as they are terrifying. As a boy in Venezuela, Jesus Rivas was struck by the beauty of them and other local wildlife. As a scientist, Dr. Rivas has made it his job to find out as much as he can about the anaconda. First he finds a snake. Then he wrestles it until the snake is so tired that it can be subdued. That usually takes 15 or 20 minutes. Rivas then restrains the snake or moves it to a place where he can take blood and tissue samples before letting it go.

Rivas has already discovered many interesting things about the anaconda. For one, the females are about five times as large as the males. When they mate, the female lets the male wrap its tail around her. Some snakes lay eggs, but anacondas give birth to live young. Their parenthood doesn't last long, though. Within a short time, the young are off hunting their own food.

Standardized Test Practice: Long Reading Passages (Grades 5–6) © 2009 by Michael Priestley, Scholastic Teaching Resources

Name _____   Date _____

Questions 1–10: Choose the best answer to each question, or write your answer on the lines provided.

1. According to the article, why is the Amazon River area an ideal place for anacondas?

Ⓐ It is warm and steamy.

Ⓑ Few people live there.

Ⓒ It has many large trees.

Ⓓ The water is very clear.

2. Which sentence from the article states an opinion?

Ⓐ The females are about five times as large as the males.

Ⓑ Anacondas are as beautiful as they are terrifying.

Ⓒ Some snakes kill by poisoning their victims with their fangs.

Ⓓ The anaconda has greenish brown scales with black spots.

3. Describe two times when an anaconda might lie very still. Explain why it is not moving in each instance. (4 points)

_____

_____

_____

_____

_____

_____

_____

4. **How are anacondas and pythons alike?**

   Ⓐ Both live in Asia.

   Ⓑ Both poison their victims.

   Ⓒ Both move very fast.

   Ⓓ Both are constrictors.

5. **"Its chief rival for the title is the reticulated python of Asia."**

   What does the word <u>rival</u> mean as it is used in this sentence?

   Ⓐ ruler

   Ⓑ author

   Ⓒ challenger

   Ⓓ enemy

6. **Where in Asia would you expect to find the reticulated python: high mountains, snow-covered plains, or warm swamps? Give a reason to support your answer. (2 points)**

_____

_____

_____

_____

7. **What clue in the article suggests that Dr. Jesus Rivas is probably very strong?**

   Ⓐ He works in bare feet.

   Ⓑ He wrestles with large snakes.

   Ⓒ He lives in South America.

   Ⓓ He wades through swampy wetlands.

Standardized Test Practice: Long Reading Passages (Grades 5–6) © 2009 by Michael Priestley, Scholastic Teaching Resources

8. "Constrictors kill by wrapping their bodies around prey and <u>squeezing</u> it."

   Which word could best replace the word <u>squeezing</u> in this sentence?

   Ⓐ crowding

   Ⓑ hugging

   Ⓒ crushing

   Ⓓ pinching

9. **According to this article, the anaconda senses smells through its —**

   Ⓐ nostrils.

   Ⓑ teeth.

   Ⓒ ears.

   Ⓓ tongue.

10. **Suppose you learned that very few snake researchers have seen an anaconda in the wild. What would be the most likely reason for this?**

    Ⓐ Anacondas are not as interesting to study as some other snakes.

    Ⓑ Anacondas live mostly in the water and are hard to find.

    Ⓒ Most snake researchers live in cold climates.

    Ⓓ People who study snakes don't visit South America.

Standardized Test Practice: Long Reading Passages (Grades 5–6) © 2009 by Michael Priestley, Scholastic Teaching Resources

Name _____   Date _____

Directions: Read "The Winter Count." Then answer questions 1–10.

The Winter Count

I sat with my mother and father and grandparents by the fire inside the tepee. We had all just enjoyed a good dinner of buffalo stew and were staring into the fire with our own thoughts when the tepee door lifted. With an icy blast of wind, my cousin, Bear Tooth, and his little sister, Bright Star, ran inside. More aunts and uncles and cousins followed, each of them paying their respects to Grandma and Grandpa as they entered. Everyone shifted to let the whole family sit, knee to knee, around the fire.

"The first snow is falling, and the year is over," Grandpa announced. "It is a good day to review the winter count of our people. Daughter, get the buffalo skin."

My mother dug carefully through our large trunk filled with things such as painted bowls and my great-grandmother's porcupine quill embroidery. The winter count is a kind of calendar kept on a large, whole buffalo skin. It shows a pictograph of a single important event from each year. Our winter count was about 100 years old, and it contained many symbols I didn't understand.

Mother held up the large roll of buffalo skin, almost as tall as herself. As Grandpa's oldest daughter, she held one side of the rolled-up skin while Grandpa pulled out the other and leaned it against the tepee wall.

"Bear Tooth, take a stick from the fire and hold it near so we can all see," Grandpa directed.

Bear Tooth and I glanced at each other briefly before he took a glowing stick from the fire. He would be 13 this year. Grandpa was recognizing that his oldest grandchild would soon become a warrior, a grown man; much would be expected of him.

"As you know," Grandpa said in his deep voice, "the winter count shows how we have survived. According to some, the Lakota should have been wiped off the face of the earth, but here we are. Every year we take out the skin and tell stories of our past. My grandfather began this count when he drew a picture of the big battle with the Crow. Many Crow warriors died, and so did some of our best Lakota men."

Standardized Test Practice: Long Reading Passages (Grades 5–6) © 2009 by Michael Priestley, Scholastic Teaching Resources

At that moment, Bright Star yanked my hair. I turned and frowned at her, but she was looking the other way as if she had done nothing.

"This one is the year the sky went crazy," said Grandpa, pointing to another picture. "One summer night when I was a boy, many stars rained down from the sky like they would come straight at us."

My uncle, Thunder Bear, politely asked what happened the year Grandpa was born.

"Ah, listen to this, and learn to bear with your family in difficult times," said Grandpa. "The year I was born, 1823, the man named Dog Ghost had such a bad quarrel with his wife that he left the camp and wandered far away. That man froze to death in a blizzard."

The adults shook their heads. Some of them muttered or sighed at this needless death.

"Here was a very bad year," Grandpa went on, pointing at a drawing of someone covered with spots and holding his stomach. There was a strange squiggle next to his stomach that I knew meant illness. "Many Lakota died of smallpox that year, including my grandfather and my sister. When my grandfather passed on, I began to keep the winter count."

Bright Star pulled my hair again so hard that I turned and slapped her knee. Grandpa frowned at me. Turning away from the hide, he addressed me and my cousins: "Why do you think we go through this every year, relating stories of the winter count?"

I stared at the ground, my face burning in embarrassment. In a small voice I said, "To learn what not to do."

"Not just that. Many people suffered before you and I came to life," Grandpa said. "We must know what they did so we can learn from them. One of the pictures shows the first Lakota Sioux who planted corn—we did not always do this. Now corn is very important to us, and some years we would have starved without it. But this is more than a bare record of the past: the winter count reveals our identity, our heart and soul. We don't want to end up like the wind blowing through the grass, a people without history. You have to know where you come from before you can decide where you're going."

"Yes, Grandpa," I said, feeling ashamed that I had made him stop his storytelling to lecture me.

"Our history is long, many times longer than this buffalo hide can hold," Grandpa continued. "The hides from before my grandfather's time have been lost, but here we have many years of our people's history. Each year the keeper meets with the elders to decide on the most memorable thing that happened that year. Then he makes a drawing to show it and adds the white man's number for that year. This skin is almost full. Soon there will be no more room on it, and I will not be here to make the new drawing or talk about the old ones. One of you will have to continue the winter count on a new piece of buffalo hide. Whoever is chosen must also know the old stories."

"I would like to be that one, the keeper of the winter count!" said Bear Tooth suddenly.

Everyone was startled to hear him speak.

"It's good to hear your enthusiasm, boy," said Grandpa with a smile. "One day you might do this, when you are a man, but you have some growing to do before that. Now I will tell you what happened the year Bear Tooth was born."

Questions 1–10: Choose the best answer to each question, or write your answer on the lines provided.

1. **Which of these events happens first in the story?**
   - Ⓐ Bright Star pulls the narrator's hair.
   - Ⓑ Bear Tooth and Bright Star enter the tepee.
   - Ⓒ The mother takes out an old buffalo skin.
   - Ⓓ Grandpa tells the story of Dog Ghost.

2. **When does this story take place?**
   - Ⓐ on a summer day
   - Ⓑ in the spring
   - Ⓒ on a winter night
   - Ⓓ in the fall

3. **This passage is an example of what literary genre?**
   - Ⓐ fantasy
   - Ⓑ historical fiction
   - Ⓒ humor
   - Ⓓ science fiction

Standardized Test Practice: Long Reading Passages (Grades 5–6) © 2009 by Michael Priestley, Scholastic Teaching Resources

4. **What happened to make Grandpa take over the role of keeping the winter count?**

   Ⓐ His grandfather died of smallpox.

   Ⓑ His father died in a blizzard.

   Ⓒ He fought bravely in a battle with the Crow.

   Ⓓ The family ran out of room on the buffalo hide.

5. **Grandpa compares people who don't know their own history to —**

   Ⓐ an empty buffalo hide.

   Ⓑ a camp during the winter.

   Ⓒ people who don't plant corn.

   Ⓓ the wind blowing through grass.

6. **You can tell from this story that Lakota children were expected to —**

   Ⓐ speak only when spoken to.

   Ⓑ show respect to their elders.

   Ⓒ become warriors at age 18.

   Ⓓ act like adults at all times.

7. **Which word best describes the mood of this story?**

   Ⓐ serious

   Ⓑ playful

   Ⓒ frightening

   Ⓓ mysterious

8. Describe the winter count and what it represents. Use details from the story. (2 points)

_____

_____

_____

_____

9. Why did the narrator feel ashamed of himself?

Ⓐ He did not understand all the symbols on the winter count.

Ⓑ He was talking to Bear Tooth instead of paying attention.

Ⓒ He interrupted Grandpa when he slapped Bright Star.

Ⓓ He did not want to become the next keeper of the winter count.

10. Describe Grandpa's relationship to the grandchildren and how he treats them. Use details from the story to support your answer. (4 points)

_____

_____

_____

_____

_____

_____

_____

Standardized Test Practice: Long Reading Passages (Grades 5–6) © 2009 by Michael Priestley, Scholastic Teaching Resources

Name _____ Date _____

Standardized Test Practice: Long Reading Passages (Grades 5–6) © 2009 by Michael Priestley, Scholastic Teaching Resources

Directions: Read "If." Then answer questions 1–7.

If

If you can keep your head when all about you
Are losing theirs and blaming it on you;
If you can trust yourself when all men doubt you,
But make allowance for their doubting too;
If you can wait and not be tired by waiting,   5
Or, being lied about, don't deal in lies,
Or, being hated, don't give way to hating,
And yet don't look too good, nor talk too wise;

If you can dream—and not make dreams your master;
If you can think—and not make thoughts your aim;   10
If you can meet with Triumph and Disaster
And treat those two impostors just the same;
If you can bear to hear the truth you've spoken
Twisted by knaves to make a trap for fools,
Or watch the things you gave your life to, broken,   15
And stoop and build 'em up with worn-out tools;

If you can make one heap of all your winnings
And risk it on one turn of pitch-and-toss,
And lose, and start again at your beginnings,
And never breathe a word about your loss;   20
If you can force your heart and nerve and sinew
To serve your turn long after they are gone,
And so hold on when there is nothing in you
Except the Will which says to them: "Hold on!"

If you can talk with crowds and keep your virtue,   25
Or walk with kings—nor lose the common touch,
If neither foes nor loving friends can hurt you,
If all men count with you, but none too much;
If you can fill the unforgiving minute
With sixty seconds' worth of distance run,   30
Yours is the earth and everything that's in it,
And—which is more—you'll be a man, my son!

—*Rudyard Kipling (1865–1936)*

Standardized Test Practice: Long Reading Passages (Grades 5–6) © 2009 by Michael Priestley, Scholastic Teaching Resources

Questions 1–7: Choose the best answer to each question, or write your answer on the lines provided.

1. **What is the speaker's message in this poem?**

   Ⓐ Don't let other people spend your money.

   Ⓑ Some people think and dream too much.

   Ⓒ Life is hard and you will have to suffer.

   Ⓓ Here is how a grownup should try to act.

2. **"If you can bear to hear the truth you've spoken**

   Twisted by <u>knaves</u> to make a trap for fools"

   What are <u>knaves</u>?

   Ⓐ cutting tools

   Ⓑ ropes or wires

   Ⓒ dishonest men

   Ⓓ angry speakers

3. **Which literary device does the poet use in this poem?**

   Ⓐ repetition

   Ⓑ dialogue

   Ⓒ flashback

   Ⓓ exaggeration

4. **"If you can <u>keep your head</u> when all about you**

   Are losing theirs and blaming it on you"

   What is another way to say <u>keep your head</u>?

   Ⓐ be happy

   Ⓑ remember words

   Ⓒ stay calm

   Ⓓ protect secrets

5. **The speaker of this poem would most likely agree that —**

   Ⓐ you should do the right thing even if other people do not.

   Ⓑ you have to build your home with your own two hands.

   Ⓒ you should always do what your family expects you to do.

   Ⓓ you can't please everyone all the time, but you should try.

6. **Who is the speaker in this poem?**

   Ⓐ a student

   Ⓑ a good friend

   Ⓒ a brother

   Ⓓ a father

7. **What is the speaker trying to say in lines 17–20? Explain the main point of these lines. (2 points)**

_____

_____

_____

_____

Standardized Test Practice: Long Reading Passages (Grades 5–6) © 2009 by Michael Priestley, Scholastic Teaching Resources

Name _____ Date _____

Directions: Read "The Great Mayan Civilization." Then answer
questions 1–10.

The Great Mayan Civilization

Centuries ago, a group of people called the Maya built a great
civilization. They lived in parts of present-day Mexico and Central
America. They left behind huge ruins and other signs of a fascinating
culture. Every day, scholars learn more about the Maya, who first arrived
in the area about 1200 BCE. Some descendants of the Maya still live
there today.

The earliest Maya settled in small, scattered villages in both the
lowlands and the mountains. They lived in the jungles, on open lands,
and near the coast. They were mainly farmers. Their crops included
maize (corn), squash, beans, chili peppers, and cacao. The Maya raised
a few kinds of animals for food. They also hunted for
wild game and gathered eggs and honey. Those
who lived near the ocean included fish, other
seafood, and seabirds in their diet.

The Maya were skillful in weaving,
pottery, basketry, and stone carving.
They made most of what they needed
for everyday life. They also created
items for decorative, religious, and trade
purposes. Their early houses were simple
homes made of poles covered with thatch (dried
plants). However, they also had the skills to build huge pyramids, which
were used for religious rites. The oldest of these amazing structures date
to about 400 BCE. Later, the Maya built other large buildings, such as
palaces for their rulers.

Early settlements were organized by kinship, or families. Each one
was headed by a chief. Over time, many of these settlements grew into
large city-states. They were ruled by kings, who also served as priests. A
few of the ancient Mayan cities were as big as modern cities. For example,
the ruins of Tikal cover an area of 10 square miles (25 sq km) and include
more than 4,000 structures. The "greater Tikal area" may have been 10
times that size with more than 90,000 residents.

The Mayan city-states traded with one another, using cacao beans as a kind of money. They traded for feathers, dyes, jade, obsidian, furs, salt, cloth, incense, and food. People carried these goods long distances in backpacks or canoes. (The Maya did not use wheeled carts or pack animals.) The cities also made war on each other sometimes.

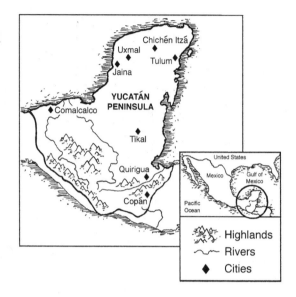

As time went on, Mayan society split into several classes. These included priest-kings, nobles, commoners, and slaves. The different classes were known by their clothes, hair styles, and tattoos. They also led very different kinds of lives. The priest-kings and nobles were the upper classes. They lived in great luxury with fine houses and nice clothing. Commoners had to give large amounts of both labor and goods for their support. The nobles also held slaves, who were often killed when the masters died. That way, it was supposed, the slaves could continue to serve their masters in the afterlife.

Religion was central to Mayan life. The Maya worshiped a number of gods. These gods were connected with rain, maize, the sky, and other parts of the natural world. The Maya believed they had to make offerings to these gods at very precise times during the year. This belief led to one of the Maya's most amazing inventions: the calendar. Today we take calendars for granted, but creating an accurate calendar is hard to do. It requires the careful study of the sun, moon, and stars and the use of advanced math. The Maya actually had several kinds of calendars with different uses.

The Maya also had a writing system. It was developed as early as 300 BCE. The system used marks, pictures, and symbols. These marks have been found written on paper made from tree bark, carved into roof beams and large stone pillars, and painted on pottery. Scholars have not fully decoded these marks. But they do know that the Maya kept records of the stars, history, and family lines.

Somewhere between 800 and 925 CE, the Mayan civilization collapsed in most of the lowland areas. The cause may have been a natural disaster, warfare, or something else. Scholars do not know for sure. They do know that the lowland Maya stopped constructing large buildings and then abandoned their cities. Maya continued to live in the highlands and in some places close to the coast. There, contact with other groups of people

Standardized Test Practice: Long Reading Passages (Grades 5–6) © 2009 by Michael Priestley, Scholastic Teaching Resources

Standardized Test Practice: Long Reading Passages (Grades 5–6) © 2009 by Michael Priestley, Scholastic Teaching Resources

brought changes in their culture. The people began to build new styles of buildings and new crafts, and they made changes in lifestyle.

One of these new groups of people was especially important. The Putún Maya moved into the Yucatán area from the north in about 900 CE. They had lived near other native peoples of Mexico, and they brought Mexican influences with them. For example, their main god was a feathered snake. This god was common in central Mexico but unrecognized in the Yucatán area.

The Putún also had different social classes. For example, they had a separate priesthood. This was unlike other Mayan groups whose kings were also the religious leaders. Other new classes included military leaders and merchants. All of the upper classes still relied on commoners and slaves for their support.

The Putún looked different, too. In most of the Mayan culture, long thin heads and crossed eyes were considered beautiful. Upper-class Mayans shaped their babies' heads and hung objects in front of their eyes to achieve these looks. In contrast, carved images of the Putún people lack such features.

With the arrival of the Putún, trade became even more important. Merchants began traveling long ways by sea in large canoes filled with goods. They also built roads and warehouses for travel by land. The roads were guarded by soldiers. These roads allowed non-Mayans as well as Mayans to come from other areas to trade. As a result, several of the Putún cities grew into large, busy places.

During this later era, some of the Mayan groups fought with each other. Different groups wanted to take control. The result weakened the Mayan people as a whole. This weakness led to their conquest by the Spanish in the 1500s. When the Spanish armies arrived, they easily defeated the Maya. The Spanish also brought diseases, causing many deaths among the Maya. Those Mayans who survived were forced to work on farms and in mines, and to adopt Spanish ways.

The Maya did not disappear, though. Some Mayans still live in the same areas where they always have. The modern Maya speak one of several Mayan languages, often mixed with Spanish. Their traditional clothing has colorful patterns that date back hundreds of years. Some groups take full part in the culture of Mexico and Guatemala; others have remained separate from the larger culture. In both cases, the Mayans are part of a proud culture more than 3,000 years old.

Questions 1–10: Choose the best answer to each question, or write your answer on the lines provided.

1. **What is the main idea of this passage?**

   Ⓐ Finding more ruins will help scholars better understand the ancient Maya.

   Ⓑ The Mayan culture is very old and has its roots in a great civilization.

   Ⓒ Today, many Mayans take part in modern cultures of Mexico and Guatemala.

   Ⓓ The great Mayan civilization collapsed over 1,000 years ago.

2. **The Mayan nobles were able to live in great luxury because they —**

   Ⓐ made offerings to the gods.

   Ⓑ wore distinctive clothing and hair styles.

   Ⓒ bought goods from other countries.

   Ⓓ were supported by commoners and slaves.

3. **Which evidence supports the idea that the Maya developed an advanced civilization?**

   Ⓐ They invented a calendar.

   Ⓑ They lived in thatched huts.

   Ⓒ They grew corn, squash, and beans.

   Ⓓ They lived in the highlands and lowlands.

4. **"Scholars have not fully <u>decoded</u> these marks."**

   Since the root word of <u>decoded</u> is "code," what does <u>decoded</u> mean?

   Ⓐ learned to make

   Ⓑ figured out the meaning of

   Ⓒ made copies of

   Ⓓ been able to discover

Standardized Test Practice: Long Reading Passages (Grades 5–6) © 2009 by Michael Priestley, Scholastic Teaching Resources

5. "This god was common in central Mexico but <u>unrecognized</u> in the Yucatán area."

What is the meaning of <u>unrecognized</u>?

Ⓐ known before

Ⓑ well known

Ⓒ not known

Ⓓ known again

6. **The passage says that the Putún Maya did not have long thin heads and crossed eyes. What does this fact suggest about the Putún?**

Ⓐ They were less intelligent than other Mayan groups.

Ⓑ They lived long before the other Mayan groups.

Ⓒ They did not admire these features.

Ⓓ They did not know how to shape a baby's head and eyes.

7. **Describe the changes that took place when the Putún Maya moved into the Yucatán area. Use details from the passage to support your answer. (4 points)**

_____

_____

_____

_____

_____

_____

_____

8. According to the map, which Mayan city was located in the highlands?

Ⓐ Copán

Ⓑ Jaina

Ⓒ Tikal

Ⓓ Comalcalco

9. Compared to the people of Uxmal (as shown on the map), the people of Tulum were more likely to —

Ⓐ have seafood in their diet.

Ⓑ experience hurricanes.

Ⓒ have gods associated with fire.

Ⓓ follow a religion.

10. Suppose you wanted to visit some of the ruins of Mayan cities. Name two reference sources you would need to help plan where you would go, and tell what kinds of information you would get from each source. (2 points)

_____

_____

_____

_____

Standardized Test Practice: Long Reading Passages (Grades 5–6) © 2009 by Michael Priestley, Scholastic Teaching Resources

Name _____ Date _____

Standardized Test Practice: Long Reading Passages (Grades 5–6) © 2009 by Michael Priestley, Scholastic Teaching Resources

Directions: Read "Flying High." Then answer questions 1–10.

Flying High

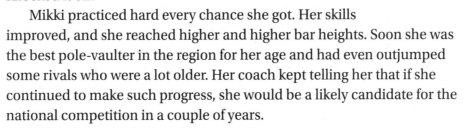

Mikki's ambition was to be the best pole-vaulter on the planet. When she was six, she watched the Olympic jumpers via satellite TV. Ever since then, she had longed to soar through the air the way they did. As soon as she was old enough, she talked her parents into signing her up for vaulting lessons with the Atlantis Track and Field Club. There she learned how to grip the pole, set her starting point, plant the pole, and take off. She worked hard to master the swing, extension, turn, and other movements for getting her body up and over the bar. She enjoyed the feeling of dropping down into the spongy foam mat after a good jump. She also knew how to dodge the falling bar when she missed the jump and knocked it off.

Mikki practiced hard every chance she got. Her skills improved, and she reached higher and higher bar heights. Soon she was the best pole-vaulter in the region for her age and had even outjumped some rivals who were a lot older. Her coach kept telling her that if she continued to make such progress, she would be a likely candidate for the national competition in a couple of years.

One day, Mikki arrived home from practice to find her parents waiting impatiently on the sofa. They were holding a packet covered in strange-looking stamps.

"It's from the United States," her father pointed out as he handed it to her.

The United States? Confused, Mikki tore open the envelope. Then her jaw dropped as she read the letter inside.

"I'm invited to a special camp with a track club in the U.S.," she said wonderingly. "They want me to come for three weeks this summer, and they'll pay my expenses. They'll pay Coach's way, too." She looked up to see that her mother had turned pale. "What is it, Mami?" she asked.

"The United States is so far away," her mother replied. "It's a wonderful opportunity, and I'm so proud. But I'm worried about you traveling such a distance, even with Coach to accompany you."

"We'll have to look into it further," agreed Mikki's father.

Over the next several days, Mikki's mother and father certainly investigated. They met with her coach numerous times and e-mailed the camp for more information. They asked Mikki what she wanted to do. They changed their minds countless times but finally decided she could go.

For the next week, Mikki was so excited that she couldn't concentrate. She missed jump after jump at practice. She eventually settled down, though, and worked harder than ever.

The day finally came for Mikki and Coach to travel to America. The flight seemed to take forever, but at last they landed in a state called Indiana. They were met at the airport by a camp agent, who led them outside to a waiting van.

As they emerged from the building, Mikki looked up and gasped. She had never seen a blue sky. The sky back home ranged from pale yellow to dark orange. The vehicles on the roadway were another surprise. Even though she had watched programs about Earth on TV, actually seeing cars and buses rolling on wheels instead of scooting along on air jets was an odd experience.

For the whole trip from the airport to the track facility, Mikki kept her nose pressed to the van window. When they arrived, however, all was familiar: the oval track, the hurdles, the long-jump pit, and of course the pole-vault area. Mikki was eager to get started, but Coach insisted that she first have 24 hours of rest. (That was something else new: Earth's timekeeping system with its days and hours.)

After a good long sleep and a tasty Earth breakfast, Mikki took her pole out to the track. As she warmed up with a couple of laps around the track, she noticed that her body felt a little strange. It was probably due to stiffness and jet lag from her long flight. She did some more stretches and then picked up her pole and got ready for her first vault. She set her starting point, hoisted the pole into position, and started down the runway. As her feet left the ground, Mikki realized that this was going to be like no other jump she had ever made. She flew up, up, way past the bar, which was set at her usual height. It really felt like flying, but it was also scary—she had never been so high! The trip down to the mat felt weird, too. It was a lot slower than she was used to, and she had trouble positioning her body for landing.

Mikki noticed that other vaulters had stopped their warm-ups and were staring at her. Her own coach and the local trainers ran over in great excitement. They watched closely as Mikki started another jump and again reached a great height before starting downward.

"It must be the gravity difference," said one of the local kids. "Your planet exerts a greater pull, and your muscles are used to that. Here, with less gravity, you can really take off. Plus, our thinner air gives less

Standardized Test Practice: Long Reading Passages (Grades 5–6) © 2009 by Michael Priestley, Scholastic Teaching Resources

resistance, so you can sprint faster and jump higher. I've never seen anything like it!" The other trainers all nodded.

In spite of her amazing jumps, Mikki was very unhappy by the end of the first week of camp. The program was designed for top athletes to share their skills and learn from each other, but the other vaulters were jealous. They had no idea how scary it was for Mikki to fly so high into thin air, unsure of her control. They didn't see her breathe deeply with relief each time she landed without mishap. All they saw was the attention she was getting.

Coach found Mikki crying in their room one evening and asked her what was bothering her. Coach had not realized how worried Mikki was, or how lonesome she felt. She assured Mikki that she was watching carefully and would not allow her to get hurt. She also told Mikki how they could adapt this Earth experience to Mikki's training back home. Over the next few days, Coach helped Mikki place interplanetary calls to her parents. She also found some girls who were willing to set aside their envy and make friends. All of that helped tremendously, and Mikki enjoyed most of her remaining time at the camp.

Before departing for home on the last day, Mikki and her new friends hugged and promised to stay in touch. They could e-mail and send pictures. Maybe someday they would even travel to her planet! "And when you're competing in the Olympics in four years," they told her, "we'll be there to watch!"

"Let's hope the host planet has this kind of gravity," Mikki smiled. "I can really fly here!"

She and Coach passed through the doors into the boarding area and were soon on their way home. As they hurtled through space, Mikki thought about the Olympics and wondered if she really might be good enough. Winning would mean she was the best pole-vaulter in the galaxy!

Whoa, girl, she said to herself, slow down! Concentrate for now on being the best on the planet.

With that thought, she drifted off to sleep and dreamed of clearing new heights under an orange-yellow sky.

Standardized Test Practice: Long Reading Passages (Grades 5–6) © 2009 by Michael Priestley, Scholastic Teaching Resources

Questions 1–10: Choose the best answer to each question, or write your answer on the lines provided.

1. **Which sentence gives a clue that this story is science fiction?**

   Ⓐ When she was eight, Mikki watched the Olympic vaulters via satellite TV.

   Ⓑ As soon as she was old enough, Mikki talked her parents into signing her up for vaulting lessons with the Atlantis Track and Field Club.

   Ⓒ Even though Mikki had watched programs about Earth on TV, actually seeing cars and buses rolling on wheels instead of scooting along on air jets was an odd experience.

   Ⓓ Mikki was eager to get started, but Coach insisted that she first have 24 hours of rest.

2. **Which sentence best describes Mikki's attitude toward pole-vaulting on her home planet?**

   Ⓐ She loves the sport and works hard to improve her skills.

   Ⓑ She enjoys flying through the air but does not like landing.

   Ⓒ She is very good and does not need to practice much.

   Ⓓ She used to enjoy the sport but now feels too much pressure.

3. **The story begins, "Mikki's ambition was to be the best pole-vaulter on the planet. When she was six, she watched the Olympic jumpers via satellite TV."**

   Explain how some of the information in these sentences turns out to have a different meaning as the story goes along. (2 points)

   _____

   _____

   _____

   _____

Standardized Test Practice: Long Reading Passages (Grades 5–6) © 2009 by Michael Priestley, Scholastic Teaching Resources

4. **At the camp in the United States, why was Mikki able to vault higher than ever before?**

    (A) Having so many people watching made her perform better than usual.

    (B) The camp had much better equipment than she had at home.

    (C) She had trained long and hard to get ready for her trip to the United States.

    (D) The gravity on Earth was different from the gravity on her home planet.

5. **"As they <u>emerged</u> from the building, Mikki looked up and gasped."**

    Which word means the opposite of <u>emerged</u>?

    (A) entered

    (B) landed

    (C) warmed

    (D) pressed

6. **Explain why Mikki was unhappy at the camp and what her coach did to help her. Use details from the story to support your answer. (4 points)**

    _____

    _____

    _____

    _____

    _____

    _____

    _____

7. "Over the next few days, Coach helped Mikki place <u>interplanetary</u> calls to her parents."

The word <u>interplanetary</u> means —

Ⓐ across the planet.

Ⓑ between planets.

Ⓒ around a planet.

Ⓓ without planets.

8. Which is the best reason to believe that Mikki is a very good pole-vaulter?

Ⓐ She has a personal coach.

Ⓑ Her friends tell her she will be on TV someday.

Ⓒ She gets invited to a special training camp.

Ⓓ Her parents let her travel to the United States.

9. Which word best describes Mikki's coach?

Ⓐ ambitious

Ⓑ encouraging

Ⓒ careless

Ⓓ affectionate

Standardized Test Practice: Long Reading Passages (Grades 5–6) © 2009 by Michael Priestley, Scholastic Teaching Resources

10. **Fill in the story chart for "Flying High." (4 points)**

TITLE "Flying High"
MAIN CHARACTERS
SETTING **Beginning**　　　　　　　　　**Middle**　　　　　　　　　**Ending**
PLOT **Beginning**
Middle
Ending

Answer Key

Passage 1: Andruw's Latest Scheme

1. D (Analyze characters' feelings, traits, and motives)

2. B (Identify causes and effects)

3. C (Identify sequence of events)

4. D (Interpret figurative language, including idioms)

5. A (Draw conclusions and generalizations)

6. Response should include a statement about Andruw's character and a supporting detail from the passage. (2 points) Example:

   Andruw tries hard to be responsible but doesn't always think things through. He had problems with his magnet project because he jumped in without really planning, but he tried to fill the orders anyway.

   (Analyze characters' feelings, traits, and motives)

Passage 2: Shirley Chisholm: A Political Pioneer

1. D (Identify main idea and supporting details)

2. D (Analyze text structure and organization)

3. A (Distinguish word denotation and connotation)

4. B (Distinguish fact and opinion)

5. C (Evaluate evidence or information and make judgments)

6. Response should include at least two key points explaining why Chisholm was a "political pioneer." (2 points) Examples:

   • Shirley Chisholm was the first African-American woman elected to Congress.
   • When she ran for president in 1972, she paved the way for other women and minorities to run for political office.

   (Draw conclusions)

7. B (Choose appropriate reference sources to gather information)

Passage 3: Deserts of the United States

1. B (Draw conclusions)

2. C (Make inferences)

3. D (Compare and contrast information and ideas)

4. A (Analyze text structure and organization)

5. Response should describe the plant life in each of the four deserts. (4 points) Examples:

   • Great Basin—plants that can live in salty soil and/or cold temperatures, such as sagebrush and greasewood
   • Sonoran—plants, such as the saguaro cactus, that do not require a lot of water
   • Mojave—yucca plants, such as the Joshua tree, which have spiny leaves that hold in moisture and/or protect it from the sun
   • Chihuahuan—shrubs and grasses that can stand cold weather; not a lot of cacti.

   (Identify main idea and supporting details)

6. B (Use context clues to determine word meaning)

7. C (Distinguish fact and opinion)

8. D (Evaluate author's style and technique)

Passage 4: How Sun, Moon, and Wind Went to Dinner

1. C (Identify narrative point of view)

2. A (Identify synonyms and antonyms)

3. B (Recognize literary genres and their characteristics)

4. Response should describe these two events in sequence (4 points):

   • Event 2—Sun and Wind enjoy themselves without thinking of their mother, but Moon saves some food for her.
   • Event 3—When Sun, Moon, and Wind return home, Sun and Wind treat Star rudely, but Moon delivers a wonderful dinner.

   (Analyze plot)

Standardized Test Practice: Long Reading Passages (Grades 5–6) © 2009 by Michael Priestley, Scholastic Teaching Resources

5. D (Analyze characters' feelings, traits, and motives)

6. B (Identify theme)

Passage 5: Natural Disasters

1. D (Identify main idea and supporting details)

2. A (Identify causes and effects)

3. A (Evaluate author's purpose and point of view)

4. Response should include at least two details describing how natural disasters can create dangerous and destructive conditions. (2 points) Examples:

   - houses and trees topple over
   - roofs are torn off houses
   - heavy rains may cause flooding
   - a white out may make driving hazardous

   (Identify main idea and supporting details)

5. D (Distinguish fact and opinion)

6. C (Use context clues to determine word meaning)

7. B (Identify causes and effects)

8. Response should describe four differences. (4 points) Examples:

   - Hurricanes form over water; tornadoes form over land.
   - Hurricanes last for days; tornadoes last for minutes.
   - Hurricanes are common on the east coast; tornadoes are common in the Midwest.
   - Hurricanes are huge storms; tornadoes are small. Hurricanes can be predicted; tornadoes cannot.

   (Compare and contrast information and ideas)

Passage 6: Mystery Paint

1. D (Make inferences and predictions)

2. B (Identify synonyms and antonyms)

3. A (Analyze characters' feelings, traits, and motives)

4. Response should describe the problem and the solution. (2 points) Example:

   - Problem: There is paint/graffiti on the school stadium and no one knows who did it.
   - Resolution: Amanda and Marcus figure out that Brian did it, and he must wash and repaint the stadium.

   (Analyze plot)

5. D (Interpret figurative language, including idioms)

6. A (Identify causes and effects)

7. C (Analyze characters' feelings, traits, and motives)

8. C (Recognize literary genres)

Passage 7: Missing Birds

1. D (Evaluate author's purpose and point of view)

2. A (Identify synonyms and antonyms)

3. C (Identify causes and effects)

4. Response should give four similarities. (4 points) Examples:

   - They all lived on islands.
   - They were large birds.
   - They could not fly.
   - They were hunted by sailors for food.
   - They became extinct.

   (Compare and contrast information and ideas)

5. C (Identify main idea and supporting details)

6. B (Identify main idea and supporting details)

7. B (Draw conclusions)

8. Response should give one similarity and one difference. (2 points) Examples:

   - Similarities: They were once plentiful. They lived in forests. They lived in North America. Their habitats were destroyed.
   - Differences: Passenger pigeons traveled in huge numbers, but ivory-bills did not. Passenger pigeons were hunted, but ivory-bills were not.

   (Compare and contrast information and ideas)

9. A (Evaluate evidence or information and make judgments)

Standardized Test Practice: Long Reading Passages (Grades 5–6) © 2009 by Michael Priestley, Scholastic Teaching Resources

Passage 8: Harnessing Wind Power *and* Don't Spoil the Seashore

1. A   (Identify main idea and supporting details)

2. C   (Identify main idea and supporting details)

3. D   (Distinguish fact and opinion)

4. B   (Evaluate evidence or information and make judgments)

5. Response should include two ways wind energy was used in the past. (2 points) Examples:

   - People made sails for boats
   - People in the Netherlands built windmills to pump water and saw wood
   - People used windmills to mill grain on farms

   (Summarize information)

6. C   (Use context clues to determine word meaning)

7. B   (Evaluate author's purpose and point of view)

8. D   (Evaluate author's purpose and point of view)

Passage 9: "The Walrus and the Carpenter"

1. B   (Make inferences)

2. A   (Draw conclusions)

3. Response should include two reasons. (2 points) Examples:

   - The Oysters came out because the Walrus invited them to take a walk.
   - The Oysters came out because they were too young and inexperienced to realize what the Walrus had planned.

   (Analyze characters' feelings, traits, and motives)

4. C   (Analyze characters' feelings, traits, and motives)

5. Response should explain the "trick" (2 points): They pretended to invite the Oysters for a friendly walk and a chat, but then they ate all the Oysters for dinner.

(Analyze plot)

6. D   (Identify mood)

Passage 10: Baseball Magic

1. C   (Identify main idea and supporting details)

2. A   (Use context clues to determine word meaning)

3. C   (Identify narrative point of view)

4. B   (Make inferences)

5. Response should explain what the narrator meant. (2 points) Example:

   The narrator's father understood that the promise of a baseball game would help his son quit biting his nails because the boy loved baseball so much.

   (Analyze characters' feelings, traits, motives)

6. D   (Identify sequence of events)

7. D   (Identify mood)

8. Response should summarize the narrator's impressions and include at least four details from the passage. (4 points) Examples:

   - At first, he was scared he would lose his father in the huge crowd
   - It smelled bad, and he couldn't see because it was so dark.
   - When they entered the stadium, the lights and fresh air and crowd noise and green grass were exciting.
   - He noticed the microphone over the crowd and the big clock on the wall.
   - He was thrilled to see the famous players, to be part of the crowd, and to see his team win.

   (Summarize information)

Passage 11: The Brotherhood of the Rails *and* Steam Train Maury, King of the Hobos

1. B   (Evaluate author's purpose and point of view)

2. Response should include four details about hobo life. (4 points) Examples:

Standardized Test Practice: Long Reading Passages (Grades 5–6) © 2009 by Michael Priestley, Scholastic Teaching Resources

- Hobos try to stay clean.
- They have big meetings or conventions.
- They elect a king and queen of the hobos.
- They catch rides on trains.
- Many hobos liked life on the road; they would rather not settle down.
- Hobos were often good at getting wild food.
- Hobos formed a kind of family or brotherhood and looked out for one another.
- A hobo camp was called a jungle.

(Compare and contrast information and ideas)

3. D   (Identify main idea and supporting details)

4. D   (Interpret figurative language, including idioms)

5. A   (Identify cause and effect)

6. B   (Evaluate author's purpose and point of view)

7. C   (Use knowledge of root words, etymology, and affixes to determine word meaning)

8. A   (Identify sequence of events)

9. Response should include at least two things that Maury did. (2 points) Examples:

- He traveled by car with his wife.
- They went to hobo events.
- He visited friends in hospitals and prisons.
- He wrote a book.

(Summarize information)

10. D   (Evaluate evidence and make judgments)

Passage 12: A Very Big Snake

1. A   (Identify causes and effects)

2. B   (Distinguish fact and opinion)

3. Response should describe two times when an anaconda lies still and give a reason for each instance. (4 points) Examples:

- Anacondas lie very still when they are hunting so they can hide from their prey and take it by surprise.
- Anacondas lie still after a large meal, probably because their energy is being

used for digesting or because they are too full to move.

(Identify main idea and supporting details)

4. D   (Compare and contrast information and ideas)

5. C   (Use context clues to determine word meaning)

6. Response should identify "warm swamps" and give a reason. (2 points) Example:

The python probably lives in a warm area because it is big and it's a constrictor, like the anaconda, and it is cold-blooded.

(Draw conclusions and generalizations)

7. B   (Make inferences)

8. C   (Identify synonyms and antonyms)

9. D   (Identify main idea and supporting details)

10. B   (Evaluate evidence and make judgments)

Passage 13: The Winter Count

1. B   (Identify sequence of events)

2. C   (Identify setting)

3. B   (Recognize literary genres and their characteristics)

4. A   (Identify causes and effects)

5. D   (Analyze author's style and technique)

6. B   (Draw conclusions and generalizations)

7. A   (Identify mood)

8. Response should describe the winter count and what it represents. (2 points) Example:

- The winter count is a buffalo skin, or a record, that contains pictures of important events in the history of a tribe or a people.
- One person draws the pictures and learns the story that goes with each picture.

(Summarize information)

9. C   (Analyze characters' feelings, traits, and motives)

10. Response should describe two aspects of Grandpa's relationship with the

grandchildren and give at least two details from the story. (4 points) Example:

- Grandpa loves the grandchildren and values their role in the family, but he also expects a lot from them.
- He is nice to the grandchildren, but he expects them to listen to him.
- He shows he cares about them by helping them learn their own tribe's history.
- He also shows respect for the children's growth, as when he chooses Bear Tooth to hold the light.

(Analyze characters' feelings, traits, and motives)

Passage 14: "If"

1. D (Identify theme)

2. C (Use context clues to determine word meaning)

3. A (Recognize literary devices)

4. C (Interpret figurative language, including idioms)

5. A (Evaluate author's purpose and point of view)

6. D (Identify narrative point of view)

7. Response should explain lines 17–20. (2 points) Example:

A man should be willing to risk everything he has gained, knowing that he might lose it. If he loses, he should start over without complaining or whining about the loss.

(Draw conclusions and generalizations)

Passage 15: The Great Mayan Civilization

1. B (Identify main idea and supporting details)

2. D (Identify causes and effects)

3. A (Evaluate evidence or information and make judgments)

4. B (Use knowledge of root words, etymology, and affixes to determine word meaning)

5. C (Use knowledge of root words, etymology, and affixes to determine word meaning)

6. C (Make inferences and predictions)

7. Response should describe at least four changes that took place. (4 points) Examples:

- The Putún Maya brought new gods and religious practices; they added new social classes (including military and merchants).
- They had a separate priesthood.
- Trade became more important.
- Cities grew.

(Compare and contrast information and ideas)

8. A (Use text features and graphic features to gather information)

9. A (Use text features and graphic features to gather information)

10. Response should name two reference sources and the information they would provide. (2 points) Example:

- An encyclopedia, to identify the names of Mayan cities with ruins
- An atlas, to find the locations of the cities.

(Choose appropriate reference sources to gather information)

Passage 16: Flying High

1. C (Recognize literary genres and their characteristics)

2. A (Analyze characters' feelings, traits, and motives)

3. Response should explain two details that have a different meaning. (2 points) Examples:

- The "planet" refers to someplace other than Earth.
- The "Olympics" are an interplanetary competition.
- "Satellite TV" is not the kind of TV we have today on Earth.

(Analyze literary devices)

4. D (Identify causes and effects)

5. A (Identify synonyms and antonyms)

Standardized Test Practice: Long Reading Passages (Grades 5–6) © 2009 by Michael Priestley, Scholastic Teaching Resources

6. Response explains why Mikki was unhappy and what Coach did to help her. (4 points) Example:

- Mikki hadn't made any friends and was worried about getting hurt.
- Mikki's coach reassured her, talked to her about training back at home, helped her call her parents, and found some other kids she became friends with.

(Analyze characters' feelings, traits, and motives)

7. B   (Use knowledge of root words, etymology, and affixes to determine word meaning)

8. C   (Evaluate evidence or information and make judgments)

9. B   (Make inferences)

10. Response should be a completed story chart. (4 points) Example:

TITLE "Flying High"
MAIN CHARACTERS Mikki, Mikki's parents, Coach
SETTING   **Beginning** **Middle** **Ending**   Mikki's Earth (training a spaceship   planet camp in   Indiana)
PLOT   **Beginning**   Mikki gets invited to camp in the U.S. for pole-vaulting.   Her parents are worried but eventually let her go.
Middle   Mikki and Coach arrive in the U.S.   When Mikki tries pole-vaulting, she goes much higher than she expected. This brings her a lot of attention and makes the other vaulters jealous.   Coach discovers that Mikki is unhappy and takes steps to make her feel better.
Ending   Mikki says goodbye to her friends and heads for home.

(Identify plot)

Student Scoring Record

Student Name _____ Grade _____

Teacher Name _____ Class _____

Directions: Write the total number of points the student earned on each passage. To calculate the percent score, divide the number of points earned by the total number of points. Then multiply by 100. For example, a student who earns 6 out of 8 points has a score of 75% (6 ÷ 8 = 0.75 × 100 = 75%).

Passages	Number of Points/Total	Percent (%)
1. Andruw's Latest Scheme	7	
2. Shirley Chisholm: A Political Pioneer	8	
3. Deserts of the United States	11	
4. How Sun, Moon, and Wind Went to Dinner	9	
5. Natural Disasters	12	
6. Mystery Paint	9	
7. Missing Birds	13	
8. Harnessing Wind Power *and* Don't Spoil the Seashore	9	
9. "The Walrus and the Carpenter"	8	
10. Baseball Magic	12	
11. The Brotherhood of the Rails *and* Steam Train Maury	14	
12. A Very Big Snake	14	
13. The Winter Count	14	
14. "If"	8	
15. The Great Mayan Civilization	14	
16. Flying High	17	

Standardized Test Practice: Long Reading Passages (Grades 5–6) © 2009 by Michael Priestley, Scholastic Teaching Resources